Lincoln Christian College

The Teaching of Ethics I

The Teaching of Ethics in Higher Education

A Report by The Hastings Center

INSTITUTE OF
SOCIETY, ETHICS AND
THE LIFE
SCIENCES THE
HASTINGS
CENTER

D0922461

Copyright © 1980 by the Institute of Society, Ethics and the Life Sciences

All rights reserved. No part of this book may be reproduced or transmitted in any form or by any means, electronic or mechanical, including photocopying, recording or by any information storage and retrieval system, without permission in writing from the Publisher.

The Hastings Center
Institute of Society, Ethics and the Life Sciences
360 Broadway
Hastings-on-Hudson, New York 10706

Library of Congress Cataloging in Publication Data

Hastings center.
    The teaching of ethics in higher education.
    (The Teaching of ethics ; 1)
    Bibliography: p.
    1. Ethics—Study and teaching (Higher)—United
States. I. Title. II. Series: Teaching of ethics ; 1.
BJ66.H37   1980   170'.7'1173   80–10294
ISBN 0–916558–09–6

Contents

64643

Preface

Since its founding in 1969, The Hastings Center (Institute of Society, Ethics and the Life Sciences) has worked to shed light on ethical issues in contemporary society—especially in biology, medicine, and the behavioral sciences—and to encourage informed and articulate debate about them. Its founders were convinced that the central problems posed by rapid advances in the biological, medical, and behavioral sciences are ethical; and they believed that these problems should be approached through careful interdisciplinary inquiry and well-developed educational programs.

One of the Center's first goals was to encourage the teaching of bioethics to future physicians. A decade ago, medical schools were doing very little to prepare their students to cope with the personal and professional moral problems they would almost surely encounter in their later practice. The last ten years have seen a dramatic change. The field of bioethics, despite initial suspicion and objections from many quarters, is now well underway, with serious courses being offered in about half of the medical schools in the United States, in many schools of nursing and allied health care, and by the hundreds at the undergraduate level. At the same time, a strong scholarly literature on the subject has developed, many teachers now specialize in the subject, and financial and other forms of support are forthcoming.

Yet by the mid-seventies it had become obvious that the interest in bioethics was only one sign of a much wider concern with the teaching of ethics in higher education. Increasing perplexity was being expressed in all of the professions about the moral problems of their work and the deficiencies of professional schools in preparing their students to meet them. At the undergraduate level, efforts were underway to find better ways for students to encounter ethical or value problems as a way of offsetting the strong trends toward specialization and job-oriented curriculums. The "core curriculum" movement sought ways to include the dimension of ethics and values as a central ingredient. The interest that Lawrence Kohlberg and others engendered in the topic of "moral education" was beginning to find its way into many college courses and curriculums.

In spite of this obvious and growing interest, no single group had attempted to analyze and assess the many recent developments in the teaching of ethics. In 1977, a number of colleagues in bioethics and in other fields of ethics suggested that The Hastings Center undertake such a study. Its experience with bioethics, it was suggested, could be useful for other fields and their experience helpful to us.

In the spring of 1977, the Rockefeller Brothers Fund awarded The Hastings Center a planning grant to prepare the groundwork for a full study of the teaching of ethics in American higher education. That phase began with a systematic survey of the available literature on the teaching of ethics, a series of consultations with those in a large number of fields already teaching ethics, and an attempt to identify the most important problems and issues. At that time, it was agreed that the study should be carried out by a standing group of teachers and others with significant experience in the teaching of ethics, but that it should also be supplemented by consultants with a general concern for the state of American universities and the professions. It was important also that those carrying out the study should represent a wide range of teaching experience, and that they represent different viewpoints and types of educational institutions.

In the fall of 1977, the Carnegie Corporation of New York awarded The Hastings Center a grant to carry out a full two-year study of the teaching of ethics in American higher education. Over the course of the two years, ten extended meetings were held, a summer workshop of 150 participants was conducted at Princeton University (July, 1979), thirty papers and independent studies were commissioned, a large file of syllabi and curriculum material was accumulated, visits were paid to a number of schools, letters containing course information and opinions on the teaching of ethics were received from well over 1,000 teachers, talks were held with the officers of a number of professional and educational organizations, and advice on the project was sought from all quarters.

The Report that follows is an outcome of that work. It sets forth the issues we found to be central to the teaching of ethics, as well as its history and present status in American higher education. It also presents our conclusions on the major questions we believe should be confronted by anyone teaching ethics or by those in an administrative or policymaking position to assess that teaching. We did not try to achieve a tight, precise consensus among ourselves, only a general agreement; no member of our project would necessarily agree with every sentence in this Report. We felt we neither could nor should lay out a number of hard-and-fast prescriptions for the teaching of ethics. But we did study the issues, talked and argued at length for over two years, and came to a number of general conclusions. It is those conclusions we present here.

This Report draws upon many sources. The most important are the various papers, surveys, and studies commissioned for the project. We wish to thank their authors both for writing them and for allowing them to be subjected to the analysis and criticism they received at our meetings. A number of those papers appear in a companion volume, *Ethics Teaching in Higher Education* (New York: Plenum Press, 1980), and in a set of monographs published by The Hastings Center. We urge all readers of this Report who wish to examine the issues touched upon here in greater depth and detail to consult that book and the monographs. They are listed in the Bibliography, p. 91.

The second source of material was the extensive file of information accumulated by The Hastings Center over the course of the project and the files of those who took part in our work. The third source was the rapidly growing literature both on the teaching and the substance of ethics. The final sources of information were the many consultations and visits carried out during the course of the project, together with the hundreds of letters and syllabi we received.

We would like to thank the Rockefeller Brothers Fund for its planning grant and the Carnegie Corporation of New York for its two-year grant that allowed us to carry out the full study. To those many hundreds of faculty members who sent us letters, syllabi, and bibliographies, we can only say that they were indispensable. We very much appreciated the help of various officers of a number of professional organizations: the American Historical Association, the American Philosophical Association, the Modern Language Association, the American Council of Learned Societies, the Society for Values in Higher Education, the Association for Moral Education, and the American Association of Colleges.

A special debt of gratitude is owed to David Riesman, who followed our project with care, commented at length on our work and on particular papers, and alerted us along the way to people, events, and trends. Peter Caws, James M. Gustafson, Richard L. Morrill, Norman E. Bowie, Gene Outka, and Marvin Bressler were of great help at a meeting devoted to criticizing an early draft of this Report.

Finally, we would like to thank most heartily those who attended our meetings, wrote papers and carried out studies for us, and served as critics and commentators on the papers written by others. None of those who provided us with information or consulted with us are to be held responsible for any errors or mistaken judgments that may appear in this Report. Nevertheless, we do hope they will be willing to take partial responsibility for whatever of value the Report may contain.

Ruth Macklin, Arthur Caplan, and Carola Mone of The Hastings Center deserve special praise for their work on the project. Elizabeth Bartelme ably and efficiently lent us her editorial skills.

The list of contributors to the project include those who were permanent members of the group that carried out this study and are responsible for this Report, those who wrote papers or carried out specific studies for us, and those who took part in the series of meetings held over a period of two-and-one-half years.

Daniel Callahan   Sissela Bok
Project Co-Directors

Contributors to the Teaching of Ethics Project

A. Members of The Hastings Center Project on the Teaching of Ethics

Those listed in this category are responsible for the Report that follows.

Project Co-Directors
Daniel Callahan, Director, The Hastings Center

Sissela Bok, Lecturer, The Harvard-MIT Division of Health Sciences and Technology

Advisory Group
Derek Bok, President, Harvard University

George Bonham, Executive Director, Council on Learning; Editor-in-Chief, *Change*

Paul Freund, Carl M. Loeb University Professor Emeritus, Harvard Law School

Martin Trow, Director, Center for Studies in Higher Education, University of California, Berkeley

Hastings Center Participants
Arthur Caplan, Associate for the Humanities

Ruth Macklin, Associate for Behavioral Studies

Carola Mone, Research Assistant

Project Group Members
Robert J. Baum, Director, Center for the Study of the Human Dimensions of Science and Technology, Rensselaer Polytechnic Institute

Clifford G. Christians, Assistant Professor of Communications, University of Illinois at Urbana-Champaign

K. Danner Clouser, Professor of Humanities, Pennsylvania State University College of Medicine

Catherine L. Covert, Professor of Journalism, Syracuse University

Joel L. Fleishman, Vice Chancellor, Director, Institute of Policy Sciences and Public Affairs, Duke University

Andrew Kaufman, Professor of Law, Harvard Law School

Michael J. Kelly, Dean, University of Maryland School of Law

William F. May, Professor of Religious Studies, Indiana University

Bruce L. Payne, Lecturer, Institute of Policy Sciences and Public Affairs, Duke University

Charles W. Powers, Vice President for Public Policy, Cummins Engine Company

Dennis Thompson, Professor, Department of Politics, Princeton University

David Vogel, Associate Professor, Graduate School of Business Administration, University of California, Berkeley

Donald P. Warwick, Fellow, Harvard Institute for International Development

B. Contributors of Papers and Studies

Kurt Baier, Professor of Philosophy, University of Pittsburgh

Robert J. Baum, Director, Center for the Study of the Human Dimensions of Science and Technology, Rensselaer Polytechnic Institute

Sissela Bok, Lecturer, The Harvard-MIT Division of Health Sciences and Technology

Daniel Callahan, Director, The Hastings Center

Arthur Caplan, Associate for the Humanities, The Hastings Center

Clifford G. Christians, Assistant Professor of Communications, University of Illinois at Urbana-Champaign

K. Danner Clouser, Professor of Humanities, The Pennsylvania State University College of Medicine

Joel L. Fleishman, Vice Chancellor, Duke University; Director, Institute of Policy Sciences and Public Affairs

Paul Freund, Carl M. Loeb University Professor Emeritus, Harvard Law School

Thomas F. Green, Director, Division of Educational Foundations, School of Education, Syracuse University

Maxine Greene, Professor of Philosophy and Education, Teachers College, Columbia University

Louis W. Hodges, Director, Society and the Professions, Washington and Lee University

Michael J. Kelly, Dean, University of Maryland School of Law

Thomas Lickona, Associate Professor of Education, SUNY at Cortland

Ruth Macklin, Associate for Behavioral Studies, The Hastings Center

William F. May, Professor of Religious Studies, Indiana University

Bernard Murchland, Professor of Philosophy, Ohio Wesleyan University

Frederick A. Olafson, Professor of Philosophy, University of California at San Diego

Gene Outka, Professor of Religious Studies, Yale University

Susan Parr, Professor of English, Ithaca College

Bruce Payne, Lecturer in Policy Sciences, Institute of Policy Sciences and Public Affairs, Duke University

Charles W. Powers, Vice President for Public Policy, Cummins Engine Company

Douglas Sloan, Professor, Teachers College, Columbia University

Patricia A. Sullivan, Professor of Biology, Wells College

Dennis Thompson, Professor, Department of Politics, Princeton University

Martin Trow, Director, Center for Studies in Higher Education, University of California, Berkeley

David Vogel, Associate Professor, School of Business Administration, University of California, Berkeley

Donald P. Warwick, Fellow, Harvard Institute for International Development

C. Additional Meeting Participants

Yorke Allen, Jr., Staff Associate, Rockefeller Brothers Fund

William B. Arthur, Executive Director, National News Council

Richard Baer, Assistant Professor, Department of Natural Resources, Cornell University School of Agriculture

Stephen Bailey, Professor of Education and Social Policy, Harvard Graduate School of Education

Ronald Bayer, Associate for Policy Studies, The Hastings Center

Norman E. Bowie, Director, Center for the Study of Values, University of Delaware

James Boylan, Editor, *Columbia Journalism Review*

Marvin Bressler, Chairman, Department of Sociology, Princeton University

Sidney Callahan, Assistant Professor of Psychology, Fairfield University

James W. Carey, George H. Gallup Professor of Journalism, University of Iowa

Gerald Cavanagh, Chairman, Department of Management and Organization Sciences, School of Business Administration, Wayne State University

Peter Caws, Professor of Philosophy, CUNY Graduate Center

John Chamberlin, Associate Professor of Political Science, Institute of Public Policy Studies, University of Michigan

Carleton B. Chapman, M.D., President, The Commonwealth Fund

Harvey P. Dale, Associate Professor of Law, New York University

Gerald Dworkin, Professor of Philosophy, University of Illinois at Chicago Circle

Karin Egan, Program Associate, Carnegie Corporation of New York

John Fielder, Associate Professor of Philosophy, Villanova University

Michael Gannon, Ring Professor of Social Ethics, University of Florida

Willard Gaylin, M.D., President, The Hastings Center

Holly Goldman, Associate Professor, Department of Philosophy, University of Michigan

Jon P. Gunnemann, Associate Professor of Social Ethics, Yale Divinity School

James M. Gustafson, University Professor of Theological Ethics, University of Chicago

Kirk Hanson, Lecturer in Business Administration, Graduate School of Business, Stanford University

Gladys Hardy, National Institute of Education

Geoffrey C. Hazard, Jr., John A. Garvin Professor of Law, Yale University

J. B. Hefferlin, Editor, Higher Education, Jossey-Bass, Inc., Publishers

Louis W. Hodges, Director, Society and the Professions, Washington and Lee University

W. Michael Hoffman, Director, National Center for Business Ethics, Bentley College

David R. Hood, Director, Commonwealth Program, Carnegie Corporation of New York

Richard Hunt, Senior Lecturer in Social Studies, Harvard University

Russell E. Hurst, Executive Officer, The Society of Professional Journalists, *Sigma Delta Chi*

Franz J. Ingelfinger, M.D., Editor Emeritus, *New England Journal of Medicine*

Robert Johann, Professor of Philosophy, Fordham University

Russell Kahl, Professor of Philosophy, San Francisco State University

Herbert C. Kelman, Clarke Professor of Social Ethics, Harvard University

Kenneth Kipnis, Professor of Philosophy, University of Hawaii

Lisa Kuhmerker, Editor, *Moral Education Forum*

Edwin Layton, Professor, History of Science and Technology, Department of Mechanical Engineering, University of Minnesota

Lance Liebman, Professor, Harvard Law School

Thomas Litzenburg, Assistant Chairman, National Endowment for the Humanities

Milton Lunch, General Counsel, National Society for Professional Engineers

Jay McGowan, Dean, Fordham University

Stanley Milgram, Professor of Psychology, CUNY Graduate Center

William Lee Miller, Director, The Poynter Center, Indiana University

Kathryn Mohrman, Editor, *Forum for Liberal Education*

Mark H. Moore, Associate Professor of Public Policy, John F. Kennedy School of Government

Richard L. Morrill, President, Salem College

Bernard Murchland, Professor of Philosophy, Ohio Wesleyan University

E. L. Pattullo, Professor of Psychology, Harvard University

William G. Perry, Jr., Professor of Education and Director, Bureau of Study, Harvard University

David Pollick, Professor of Philosophy, St. John's University (Collegeville, Minnesota)

Tabitha Powledge, Associate for Biosocial Studies, The Hastings Center

David E. Price, Associate Professor of Political Science and Policy Sciences, Institute of Policy Sciences and Public Affairs, Duke University

Don K. Price, Professor of Government, John F. Kennedy School of Government

Vincent Punzo, Professor of Philosophy, St. Louis University

James R. Rest, Associate Professor, Department of Social, Psychological and Philosophical Foundations, University of Minnesota

William L. Rivers, Paul C. Edwards Professor of Communication, Stanford University

Bernard Rosen, Professor of Philosophy, Ohio State University

Kevin Ryan, Associate Dean for Program Development, College of Education, Ohio State University

Thomas Scanlon, Professor of Philosophy, Princeton University

Charles L. Scarlott, Senior Advisor, Exxon Corporation

James Schaub, Acting Director, Humanities Perspectives on the Professions, Department of Civil Engineering, University of Florida

Richard S. Sharpe, Program Officer for the Committee on Public Policy and Social Organization, The Ford Foundation

Vivien Shelanski, Editor, *Science, Technology and Human Values*

Joan Sieber, Assistant Professor of Psychology, California State University at Hayward

Allen P. Sindler, Dean, Graduate School of Public Policy, University of California, Berkeley

Margaret Steinfels, Editor, *The Hastings Center Report*

Colonel Peter L. Stromberg, Chairman, Ethics and Professionalism Committee, United States Military Academy

Colin Thomson, Faculty of Law, Australian National University

Jane Uebelhoer, Instructor, Humanities and Social Sciences, University of Missouri, Rolla

Stephen H. Unger, Professor, Department of Electrical Engineering and Computer Science, Columbia University

Robert M. Veatch, Senior Associate, The Hastings Center

Paul R. Verkuil, Dean, Tulane University Law School

Jack L. Walker, Director, Institute of Public Policy Studies, University of Michigan

Clarence Walton, Professor of Business, Columbia University

Murray Wax, Professor of Anthropology, Washington University

Preston Williams, Professor of Theology and Contemporary Change, Harvard Divinity School

Vivien Weil, Assistant Professor of Philosophy, Illinois Institute of Technology

David L. Wee, Department of English, Senior Tutor of the Paracollege, St. Olaf College

Charles Wolf, Jr., Director, The Rand Graduate Institute

Douglas Yates, Associate Dean, School of Organization and Management, Yale University

Howard M. Ziff, Professor of Journalism, University of Massachusetts-Amherst; Visiting Professor of English, Amherst College

I. Framing the Issues

A. Introduction

Despite the common observation of foreign visitors and critics that Americans are obsessed with morality, the truth is more complicated. We are heirs to a constitutional and cultural tradition deeply rooted in ethical convictions. The language of morality comes easily to American lips. That the tragedy of Watergate was cast, much to the amazement of many Europeans, in moral as well as political terms is simply one more piece of evidence about our national proclivities. Yet there has always been ambivalence as well. Our equally important American concern for freedom, our skepticism about moral consensuses, and our tradition of separation of church and state, have all tempered what otherwise might easily become ethical zealotry. We are attracted to the devising of ethical codes and principles, but suspicious of any move that might point in the direction of moral indoctrination or any ethical party line.

The ambivalence is nowhere more evident now than in American higher education. A rash of recent articles and editorials have called for a central place in the curriculum for an examination of ethical issues. Colleges and professional schools have been urged to worry about the moral and not just the cognitive development of their students. There has been a burst of "experimental" and "innovative" programs designed to introduce students to ethical and value problems, and a number of workshops, new degree programs, and textbooks have been developed to provide the background and the tools needed for the teaching of ethics.

All that activity might suggest that ethics is sweeping the collegiate landscape. That is not necessarily the case. Those working in the field of ethics regularly entertain each other with anecdotes about the indifference or hostility of colleagues, about the difficulty of persuading curriculum committees to allow an ethics course to be introduced, about rejections from foundations of proposals to develop courses, and about the problem of finding qualified teachers even when all the other hurdles have been surmounted. Great enthusiasm is bewilderingly counterpoised against an equally great lack of interest. A glance at the primary and secondary school level is perhaps suggestive of the deep national roots of the ambivalence. A June, 1978, Gallup Poll found that 84 percent of public school parents surveyed favored instruction in morality and moral behavior in the schools.[1] Only 12 percent opposed such instruction. Nonetheless, efforts to actually introduce such programs at the primary and secondary school level have usually run into enormous local resistance. While no comparable public opinion poll has been conducted concerning higher education, we would expect similar results—a general concern for ethics by no means automatically results in an eagerness to make it part of the curriculum. In some colleges and universities it will and in others it will not.

What accounts for the recent fresh concern over the teaching of ethics? No single explanation will suffice. It represents, apparently, the convergence of many cultural and academic currents. On the societal level, our newspapers and our pundits have bemoaned symptoms of a moral vacuum in our society, a sense of moral drift, of ethical uncertainty, and a withering away of some traditional roots and moorings. There is a concern about juvenile delinquency, about white-collar crime, about a culture of narcissism, about the absence of fixed and firm guidelines for both personal and institutional behavior. From the outside, almost all the professions are beset with criticisms concerning the moral behavior of their members—physicians negligent toward their patients, lawyers who engage in outright criminal activities, engineers or scientists who conceal information necessary for public safety, social scientists who systematically engage in deception to carry out research, businessmen who exploit the public, cheat the government, and worship the dollar as the only important human value. A recent Carnegie study emphasized widespread unethical practices by college students.[2] The list of public complaints is long, and the professions have seen a comparative drop in public confidence.

What, many persons ask, are our children coming to, our professionals, and our society as a whole? One need by no means take those accusations and generalizations at face value, as if everything is rotten and getting worse. Many worries are overblown, some are based upon illogical jumps made from the conduct of a few to the conduct of the many, and still more simply represent a tendency to complain about the morality of others. For all that, the very fact of such rising concern points to increased external pressures "to do something about ethics"; they represent strong symptoms of a society in the throes of considerable moral turmoil.

Yet, if many of those external complaints turn upon a perceived lack of professional and personal virtue, quite another set of issues—internal to many fields—has brought concerns about morality to the fore. They are issues that turn less on personal virtue than on the emergence of a number of exceedingly difficult ethical dilemmas, both within the society and within the professions. Tensions between freedom and justice, between individual autonomy and government regulation, between efficiency and equity, between privacy and a right to information, between the rights of individuals and the rights of society, have become more sharply focused. They have been expressed in a wide range of specific issues: abortion, termination of treatment of dying patients, whistle-blowing in the professions, conflict of interest among researchers and policymakers, questions of risks and benefits in assessing scientific, technological, and environmental issues, and the limits of paternalism in medicine, government, and the law. The list of particular problems is a long one and could be extended for pages. It represents, if not always wholly new issues, ones that have emerged much more sharply in the face of rapid technological and social change—a change that has created new institutional and personal moral dilemmas and that has left many persons bewildered and uncertain about the right course of conduct.

Within the universities, concern has been expressed that questions of personal morality and integrity are not being sufficiently addressed in the classroom, and that larger social questions of public policy, justice, freedom, and the economy are not being examined from a moral point of view. Universities and professional schools, it is held, are simply not equipping students to deal with the personal and professional moral dilemmas they will encounter in their later life. With programs that increasingly tend toward specialization, professionalism, and the imparting of technical knowledge, a wide gap has been opened where ethical and value issues should be, but are not, central. At a time when an examination of the moral life, and of concrete ethical problems, cries out for attention, events and trends in the universities and professional schools seem systematically to exclude them—and that is a source of growing worry for many.

In sum, a wide range of forces and pressures are at work within the society, within the professions, and within the universities to confront issues of ethics and morality more squarely. That much of this pressure has focused on the university is hardly surprising. Americans have always had a strong faith in the importance of education, and a no less strong belief that what happens in schools, colleges, and universities can make a decisive social difference in the lives of those who pass through them. That many persons are now calling for a more central place in the higher education curriculum for questions of ethics and morality may be seen as simply a fresh resurgence of that faith. No doubt there is at times entirely too much faith in education; many other forces influence the lives of individuals. But that so many Americans do look to universities and professional schools to prepare them for a life in the broader society points to a reasonable presumption that those schools should find a place for a serious consideration of ethics and morality.

Whatever the specific reasons, then, there can be no doubt of a fresh interest in the teaching of ethics. Within the past decade, almost every medical school in the country has initiated at least some introduction to medical ethics, and over half have very serious courses; almost 90 percent of the law schools in the United States have required courses in professional responsibility; courses on corporate responsibility are rapidly emerging in business and accounting schools; the area of science, technology, and human values has established itself at the undergraduate level; courses on ethics are being introduced in nursing schools, and the same is true of schools of journalism; major programs on engineering ethics are appearing at some of the leading schools in that field; special courses in environmental ethics, in the ethics of racial and sexual discrimination, in social science research and application, and in public policy and administration are being introduced at a very rapid rate.

At the University of Florida, 900 students a year take an interdisciplinary, introductory course in social ethics, and many more students are turned away each year. In the same university, there are courses in ethics in the medical school, the nursing school, and the school of engineering. New and rigorous courses on ethics have been introduced at the United States Military Academy and at the United States Air Force Academy. We estimate that at least 11,000–12,000 courses in ethics are currently taught at the undergraduate and professional school levels.

To be sure, courses in ethics have traditionally been offered over the years in departments of philosophy, theology, and religious studies. But the content of many of those courses has shifted in recent years toward bringing students into direct contact with specific questions of applied ethics and away from a strictly theoretical approach. No less significantly, courses and programs in ethics are appearing in places where they had not been seen before: in the professional schools, in newly devised core curriculum and humanities programs, in a number of departments outside philosophy and religion.

Yet, if all this activity signals a new interest, it is by no means uniform, either within departments or divisions of the same university or among different universities and professional schools. Probably the majority of professional schools still offer nothing of a serious and systematic nature in ethics, and hundreds of undergraduate institutions—most of which stress the importance of ethics in the introductions to their catalogues—offer little in the way of ethics other than some traditional (and usually elective) departmental offerings in philosophy and religion. At some colleges, over twenty courses in ethics can be counted in different schools and departments. In others, none at all. At some schools there is considerable enthusiasm, while at others there is indifference or outright rejection. Some teachers report student apathy toward the subject; others report enthusiasm. Some universities claim that the pressure is coming from the students for such courses, whereas others say that the pressure is coming from administrators.

Many educators are openly worried about the introduction of innovative courses into the curriculum; others will accept no other kind. Many of those teaching ethics in departments of religion and philosophy look askance at current efforts to introduce courses on ethics into other departments or into professional programs. That many applied ethics courses are taught by junior faculty members, using nontraditional interdisciplinary methods, does little to reassure discipline-oriented philosophers or theologians that substance and rigor can be preserved in the new programs. Moreover, the subject matter deemed appropriate for new courses on ethics is a source of contention. Even many of those directly involved in special programs or courses on ethics report that the scope of the field is troublesome to specify. That uncertainty may be reflected in the diverse language used to describe such courses—"values education," for instance, or "moral education," "valuing," "applied ethics," "social ethics," "professional responsibility," or "social values."

In addition to these uncertainties, some educators doubt that ethics, applied or otherwise, can be approached in any coherent theoretical way. They see ethics as an inherently "soft" subject, not amenable to rigorous study. Still others fear that repressive and dogmatic moralizing may result from the teaching of ethics. A few have argued that individuals either have a solid morality or lack it, and that little can be done in the classroom to change that situation. Moral development, they contend, has comparatively little to do with formal education, reasoning, and analysis; much more depends upon acquiring in the home or in early childhood the personal character and strength of conviction necessary to translate personal values into practice. Arjay Miller, former Dean of the Stanford Business School, expressed what is no doubt a widespread attitude toward the teaching of ethics when he said, "I believe we ought to be doing more, but I'm not sure exactly what. . . . It's a problem of motivation and basic human values. There are a lot of people in jail today who have passed ethics courses."[3]

The enthusiasm and the proliferation of new courses, coupled with the uncertainty voiced and the objections raised, all convinced us that a sober assessment of the teaching of ethics was needed.

B. The Purpose of Our Study

Our study of the teaching of ethics was conducted in order to provide such an assessment: to examine the present state of ethics teaching in the United States, to analyze the most important questions it raises, and to make recommendations concerning goals and standards.

We began the study with a conviction that ethics can and should have a significant place in the curriculum of undergraduate and professional schools. This conviction is underscored by a growing awareness of many college and professional school graduates that their education offered no opportunity for serious consideration of questions of moral choice; they now face questions for which they are unprepared. Morality is part of any reflective personal life, and ethical perspectives and deliberation shape cultural and civic life. To leave ethics out of a curriculum makes little sense.

Few would claim that the teaching of ethics offers a panacea to the moral problems either of the students or of society as a whole. Our only contention is that serious and systematic work in ethics will enable students to grapple, at a mature level, with questions they will inevitably have to face, both in their present and in their future life. Morality is, in great part, built upon rules of conduct, both negative and positive. As Michael Walzer has written, "Studying these rules is no guarantee of their effectiveness. It won't lead people to make the right moral choices, since we will continue to disagree about what the right choices are. But it may enable people to talk about moral questions more self-consciously and more openly; it may help them to make more reflective judgments; and it may compel them to defend in public the substance of what they do."[4] And as Derek C. Bok has noted, "Although the point is still unproved, it does seem plausible to suppose that the students in these courses will become more alert in perceiving ethical issues, more aware of the reasons underlying moral principles, and more equipped to reason carefully in applying these principles to concrete cases. Will they behave more ethically? We may never know. But surely the experiment is worth trying, for the goal has never been more important to the quality of the society in which we live."[5]

Perhaps the strongest reason for the *explicit* teaching of ethics in the university curriculum is that moral values, ethical principles, and general stances toward the moral life are already constantly being communicated *implicitly* in the college classroom and in the university as a whole. Moral judgments are made in courses, both by professors and students, dilemmas are often confronted, and value judgments abound. Yet that form of moral education is often casual, ad hoc, and not subject to rigorous standards. A major purpose for teaching specific courses in ethics should be to uncover hidden assumptions, unchallenged and unexamined values, and to treat the realm of morality with all of the rigor and discipline that other areas of human study and concern already receive in the university.

Though we regard the teaching of ethics as valuable in principle, we acknowledge many practical difficulties. At a time of tightening budgets, the introduction of new courses in any subject can be exceedingly difficult. In many professional schools, courses in ethics are seen as a distraction from the more important business of providing students with the technical training they need. As one physician argued, time given to a course in medical ethics can be time taken away from acquiring those skills necessary to save human lives. A dean of a school of public policy argued that the "opportunity costs" of any proposal to introduce ethics into the curriculum should be of paramount concern—if a course in ethics is to be introduced, then some other course must be dropped or the amount of time that can be given to it reduced. How can that be justified to students who come to professional schools to receive a very specific training for a future career? How can it be justified to faculty, many of whom would like to have more time devoted to their own fields, or would propose that other new subjects be introduced into the curriculum?

In many undergraduate colleges, moreover, the very price of institutional survival is an increasing specialization, toward an education that will guarantee specific jobs upon graduation. The humanities in general are feeling that pressure, and it is all that many departments can do to hold on to those few courses in the liberal arts that still remain. Any course in ethics seems, in many cases, neither feasible to administrators nor acceptable to students.

The training of those who teach ethics also raises special difficulties. Since much of the recent interest in ethics has focused on questions of applied ethics, or ethics taught in an interdisciplinary context, where can trained teachers be found? Those trained in philosophy or religion usually have no experience treating the ethical problems of other fields or disciplines, while those trained in other fields often have no background in ethics. A number of professional schools report that they would be prepared to introduce courses on ethics, but have not been successful in finding suitable teachers.

Beyond those difficulties, broad and problematic issues emerged from our study. We take them up separately in Part III of this Report. They concern:

• *Goals in the Teaching of Ethics.* It is unclear just what goals are meant to be served by the teaching of ethics, and many different viewpoints can be found. Are courses in ethics meant to improve the moral character of students, making them more virtuous and more likely to behave in ethical ways? Is the purpose of a course in ethics to change a student's behavior? Should it aim to lead students through stages of moral growth? Are courses in ethics meant to teach people only certain analytical and reasoning skills, in order that they may better analyze and understand moral dilemmas, but without necessarily changing their behavior? Is the purpose of a course in ethics to instil in students moral outrage at injustices and immorality and a zeal to change society?

• *Indoctrination and Pluralism.* A central worry about the teaching of ethics is whether it is appropriate at all to teach a course in ethics in a pluralistic society and, if so, whether that can be done without indoctrinating students in one particular moral point of view. If, in principle, our nation is committed to a variety of moral viewpoints, and to the freedom of individuals to live out different kinds of moral lives, how can one teach ethics without impinging upon that freedom? If there is no practical way a professor can deal with all moral theories and views, how can a course in ethics be fair?

• *Qualifications for the Teaching of Ethics.* Who is qualified to teach a course in ethics? Many in the professions argue that those trained in moral philosophy or moral theology have neither the technical training nor the personal experience necessary to deal with problems in their fields. Conversely, many in theology and philosophy argue that those not formally trained in ethics are unqualified to teach it. What standards should be employed in judging the qualifications of someone who wants to teach ethics?

• *Evaluation of the Teaching of Ethics.* Even those who agree that the teaching of ethics is a valuable enterprise can disagree about how such courses should be evaluated. Should courses in ethics be evaluated at all? If so, what standards should be employed in evaluating them: behavioral change, enhancement of critical awareness and analytic skills, moral fervor, a desire to change society, or an ability simply to understand and recite the variety of moral views to be found in our society or in the world?

• *Teaching Techniques and Course Organization.* What is the best way to teach ethics? By a strong use of visual aids such as films and television, by dependence on great books and the history of ethics, by a case-study method, by exercises in applied ethical thinking, or by actual experience in the marketplace or in the clinic? Should there be independent courses in ethics—in which case ethics problems may end up as simply one more pigeonhole in a curriculum? Or should ethical issues be treated in all courses—at the risk of being treated superficially and incompetently in many? How can one set standards to insure that courses on ethics are of the highest quality and academic integrity? And how can one best develop an approach to the teaching of ethics that avoids the pitfalls of the subject?

C. The Limits of Our Study

We were obliged to restrict our inquiry in order that it not exceed our resources or become too diffuse. Accordingly, we limited ourselves, first of all, to studying the teaching of ethics in *higher education:* in undergraduate, preprofessional, and professional programs. Second, we concentrated on this teaching as it has developed in the *United States*. Third, we chose to focus on *explicit instruction* in *courses* on ethics. Needless to say, such instruction must be seen in the context of university life, and indeed of life in any society. Extracurricular activities, scholarly research, faculty and student debates on moral issues, and the ways in which universities deal with such issues as discrimination or investment policy or plagiarism, all contribute to the moral atmosphere of an institution of higher education. As one observer has pointed out, the question is not *"whether* the experience of higher education contributes to the moral development of those who are exposed to it, but rather what forms that development may take, and through what mechanisms and processes it occurs."[6] Finally, our emphasis tended to fall on the broad problems and possibilities of teaching ethics rather than on the details of course organization and pedagogical techniques.[7]

Even with such limitations for our study, however, we quickly discovered a bewildering array of different approaches and emphases. It was important, not only for our own study, but also to grasp the full range of teaching activities now taking place, to specify very clearly in our own mind just where our emphasis would fall. Richard L. Morrill provided us with a very helpful "map" of the terrain. As Dr. Morrill has written, "One can refer broadly to the need for programs in ethics and values, and be understood and affirmed by the like-minded. Yet as assumptions are revealed and programs are put in place, the apparent unity begins to dissolve. One quickly finds that teaching values and ethics and fostering moral development can be seen as vastly different and even conflicting enterprises. Serious and deep confusion can easily occur at this point, as people tacitly or consciously define one method or theory as constituting the whole of moral and values education. So, commonly, Kohlberg's theories or values clarification or normative ethics or some other approach is defined as what it means to teach values and ethics. When this occurs, as now often seems to be the case, the time has come to classify and analyze the major alternatives that are being proposed."[8]

Dr. Morrill has helpfully described four different general approaches. While there is often considerable overlap among them, and while many teachers may borrow from other approaches, some basic differences in emphasis can be discerned.

1. *Values Clarification.*[9] This movement refers to a method of self-discovery by means of which a person attempts to identify and clarify his or her own personal values, and to find a way of ranking those values. A fundamental goal of this approach is to enhance personal growth and development through increased self-awareness and self-perception. Louis Raths, Merrill Hamin, Sidney Simon, Leland W. Howe, Howard Kirschenbaum, and Brian Hall have all been active in this movement.

2. *Values Inquiry and Analysis.*[10] The main goal of value analysis is to grasp the meaning and the possibility of human situations by discerning in them the values that motivate human choice and decision. A primary assumption behind values analysis is that human beings orient and justify their choices through an implicit appeal to a set of values. The recognition of those values, together with a description and assessment of them, provides a rich way of plumbing the depths of human experience. Earl McGrath has been one of the most prominent exponents of this approach. He contends that the methodology of the natural sciences has been too rigidly applied to the study of human beings. The result has been a radical separation of facts and values, and thus a very serious impoverishment of liberal and general education. It is values that lie behind the making of wise and sensitive choices, and values have simply not been emphasized enough in the higher education curriculum.

3. *Moral Development.*[11] The moral development emphasis, the most prominent form of which is closely associated with the names of Jean Piaget and Lawrence Kohlberg, approaches moral matters within the context of a broad psychological process of human growth and maturation. For Piaget and Kohlberg, cognitive moral development is understood to occur through invariant hierarchical sequences, with movement from lower to higher stages. At each stage, moral issues are framed in a different cognitive manner, and moral judgments are justified in a different way. The role of education is understood most appropriately as the fostering of an approach to moral reflection and discussion which encourages the natural movement through the different

stages. Other notions of moral development stand behind the work of several important contemporary students of higher education. William Perry, Douglas Heath, Arthur Chickering and others have examined moral development as an important facet of intellectual and personal maturation.

4. *Normative and Applied Ethics.* Normative and applied ethics generally build upon a foundation of traditional philosophical or theological inquiry in ethics. The emphasis falls heavily on developing the student's capacity for moral reasoning; an important goal with students is that of assisting them to learn better how to analyze, justify, and criticize moral arguments. Both applied and professional ethics can be seen as closely related to the more fundamental area of normative ethics. In the case of the former, the emphasis is on finding means of analyzing and resolving practical, personal, or professional dilemmas, and in the case of the latter, developing a theoretical framework which makes it possible to deal with concrete moral problems.

Our project was concerned primarily with the teaching of normative, applied, and professional ethics, and thus is most closely identified with the fourth of Dr. Morrill's categories. At the same time, parts of our own study overlap with some of the other categories and movements, and of course many of those who teach normative, applied, and professional ethics make use of such devices as the analysis of values, stress the development of awareness on the part of students about the values they hold, and seek the possibility of moral development.

D. Defining our Terms

It is important at this point to clarify what we mean by "ethics," "moral theory," "applied ethics," and "professional ethics." These words are used in so many senses that no inquiry can proceed without defining them; we have seen discussions of the teaching of ethics falter in discouragement over the variegated use of such terms.

Following common usage and tradition, we define ethics as the study of good and evil, of right and wrong, of duty and obligation in human conduct and of reasoning and choice about them.

For the purposes of this study, we do not distinguish sharply between "ethics" in that sense and "moral theory," or between the adjectives "ethical" and "moral." ("Morals" are distinguished by some from "ethics" as referring to given rules of behavior, such as "Thou shalt not commit murder," that mark particular societies, cultures, or systems of belief.)

Contemporary philosophical usage normally distinguishes ethics into three parts: descriptive ethics, metaethics, and normative ethics.[12] Descriptive ethics seeks an accurate, objective account of the actual moral behavior or beliefs of particular persons or groups; it attempts to avoid either moral judgment or moral prescription concerning the behavior or belief system studied. Metaethics examines the meanings and uses of moral terms such as "good," or "right," the analysis of moral discourse and reasoning, and the foundations upon which moral judgments are based. Normative ethics studies actual moral arguments or statements: about what instances or classes of conduct are right or wrong, good or bad, for instance; or about traits of personal character that are worthy of praise or blame; or about the justice or injustice of societies and institutions. More broadly, it is concerned with how human beings might best lead their lives, and which states of affairs ought to be furthered in society.

When, in this Report, we speak of the "teaching of ethics," we will have in mind primarily the teaching of "normative ethics." This is not to deny the value of descriptive ethics or the importance of metaethics. Indeed, the enterprise of normative ethics will eventually force the student into broader questions of metaethics (and many philosophers will deny that a sharp distinction can, in any case, be drawn between them), and descriptive ethics can often be useful in allowing students to understand the ethical theories and moral rules of different persons, professions, and cultures. But our concern in this study is with the teaching of ethics in such a way that questions of moral judgment come to the fore. What ought I to do in this or that situation when faced with a certain moral dilemma? What standards should be employed in judging the conduct of others? What general ethical principles are the most valid for judging specific rules of conduct, and what rules of conduct are appropriate in what circumstances?

Within the domain of normative ethics, we found it helpful to use the term "applied ethics." It is not a traditional term, but one coming into increasing use in the context of a new interest in personal, social, and professional ethics.

"Applied ethics" is moral inquiry directed to making *actual* choices in moral conflicts. Without being separate from normative ethics in general, it gives a much sharper focus to moral problems arising in practice. It supplements the abstract structures of normative ethics by the systematic study of concrete moral choice. It draws on ethical theory, on moral principles, on the study of methods of choice to reach or to scrutinize moral judgments. Because of its concern with concrete human problems, applied ethics is of necessity interdisciplinary.[13] It cannot ignore the psychological, political, and other factors affecting human conduct. Applied ethics studies questions of personal choice having to do, for instance, with the keeping of promises to friends, or with abortion; it also studies questions of institutional or social choice, such as the just distribution of scarce medical, economic, natural, or other resources.

"Professional ethics," finally, is a more common term. It refers to ethical inquiry about professional conduct. "Professional ethics" is therefore part of applied ethics, and hence can be looked at both from the point of view of personal moral choice or that of collective choice. Thus in business ethics—an area of professional ethics—one can consider the problems of bribery abroad as experienced by an individual businessman; but one can also look at it as an institutional or cultural practice and consider measures needed to cope with it.

In using the term "professional ethics," we do not intend to imply that the study of ethical problems encountered at work should be limited to those occupations claiming the name "profession." The question of what counts as a profession is under ceaseless debate, and one on which we take no position. We construe the term "professional ethics" broadly enough to encompass the ethical problems encountered at work, but we also recognize that some professions have a much longer and more articulate tradition of reflection on such problems than others.[14]

A number of moral conflicts cut across professional lines. Questions of lying or cheating, for example, know no professional boundaries. The conflicts inherent in paternalism or in invasions of privacy are similarly widespread; and the problem of whether to speak out regarding misconduct in one's own organization arises in many forms of work as well. We take it to be important for courses in ethics directed to future professionals to allow students to consider such problems not only from the point of view of their future profession, but from other perspectives as well.[15]

II. The History and Present Status of the Teaching of Ethics in American Higher Education

The history of the teaching of ethics in American higher education is long, interesting, and complicated and can only be roughly and broadly characterized here. And behind its history in the United States is its even broader history in Western civilization as a whole. One recalls that in the Greek academies, in the Talmudic schools, and in the medieval universities, the study of ethics, and particularly the application of ethics to specific, everyday problems, was considered a central part of education. The early American teaching of ethics reflected that Western tradition, but also added its own special ingredients.

As Douglas Sloan has noted, "Throughout most of the 19th century the most important course in the college curriculum was moral philosophy, taught usually by the college president and required of all senior students. The moral philosophy course was regarded as the capstone of the curriculum. It aimed to pull together, to integrate, and to give meaning and purpose to the student's entire college experience and course of study. In so doing it even more importantly sought to equip the graduating seniors with the ethical sensitivity and insight needed in order to put their newly acquired knowledge to use in ways that would benefit not only themselves and their own personal advancement, but the larger society as well."[16] Reflecting the influence of English and Scottish universities, the earliest American colleges accorded moral philosophy a central place in the curriculum. A guiding assumption of early American higher education was the necessity of intellectual unity among the different branches of knowledge; and it was moral philosophy that was to provide that unity.

The attention given to moral philosophy had, in the words of Sloan, a number of significant results: "First, moral philosophy became an important source of the origin and development of what later developed as political science, economics, philosophical ethics, psychology, anthropology, and sociology. Second, as these subjects split out of moral philosophy, they based much of their claims for autonomy on the very scientific status moral philosophy accorded them. Third, as these subjects became fields of study in their own right, they often carried with them the moral and ethical imperatives of moral philosophy. The later conflict within the social sciences as to whether they could remain both scientific and ethical was to become . . . one of the major questions in American higher education. The final, and in some ways the most crucial and difficult, use of moral philosophy was to help form the moral character and disposition of the individual student. This required that the student's own ethical concerns be awakened and that he or she be inspired to pursue his or her own continuing moral development. It also demanded that the theoretical underpinnings of ethics, which were a main component of the course, be presented so as to confirm students in their own ethical striving. Furthermore, it meant providing concrete examples of ethical concern and conduct in the person of the moral philosopher. . . . It was the teacher's task to exhort, admonish, and inspire students to recognize that the demands of reality were real and all-encompassing."[17]

This is not to say that moral philosophy was alone expected to help shape the student's character and to guide conduct. That was thought to be the purpose of the full college curriculum: "The entire college experience was meant to be pre-eminently an experience in character development and the moral life, as epitomized, secured, and brought to a focus in the moral philosophy course."[18]

By the 1880s, however, those courses already stood on shaky ground. It proved increasingly difficult to convey a sense of shared values except by evading some of the fundamental moral questions of the century. Thus the subject of slavery was ignored by many who taught such courses. The contrast between the bland rhetoric of the classroom and the realities outside was often great. In addition, the hope that moral philosophy might some- how unite the disparate disciplines taught in universities could not be fulfilled—less than ever as the curriculum diversified and as the social sciences split away, one after another, from philoso- phy. In every field, professional and organizational boundaries grew stronger, and with them came claims that ethical problems arising in any one field should be dealt with by specialists within the field rather than by outsiders. The growing support for "value free" inquiry kept even many specialists from devoting serious attention to ethical issues.

By the 1930s, the field of ethics itself was becoming more specialized. Courses in ethics within undergraduate departments of philosophy or religion increasingly became elective, and reached but a small percentage of the student body. Ethics be- came one more specialized discipline, mainly concerned with the intricacies of ethical theory. At the same time, but in a diffuse manner, the perennial problems of ethics came to be taken up elsewhere in the curriculum, and often retained their place in ex- tracurricular activities. In denominational schools only, courses on ethics often retained their central role, but by the early sixties even those schools sharply reflected the general trend toward spe- cialization and professionalism, usually at the expense of tradi- tional emphases. In professional schools—rarely a strong arena for focused ethical reflection in the first place—ethics had prac- tically no official place in the curriculum. The increasing isola- tion of ethics within departments of philosophy and religion, the fragmentation of the university in general, and the technical em- phasis of professional schools together conspired to push moral reflection to the sidelines.

Only during the past decade has the field of ethics experienced a resurgence, not only within philosophy and religion generally, but also within many other departments and schools within the university. What is its present status?*

*We did not attempt to carry out a full-scale empirical survey of the number or kinds of courses in ethics now being taught in American higher education, or who is teaching those courses and with what kind of training. That would have

In an effort to get a reasonably accurate quantitative profile of the present teaching of ethics, we conducted a sample survey of course listings in 1977 and 1978 college, university, and professional school catalogues.[19] The purpose of this survey was to give us a general sense of what kinds of ethics courses were being offered at what schools, to what audiences, and in which departments. We examined the catalogues of approximately one-quarter of all institutions of higher education in the United States, 623 out of 2,270, and categorized 2,757 courses concerned with ethics.

Eighty-nine of the colleges surveyed had no ethics courses listed at all. One medium-sized university, which lists in its catalogue its final objective for students as "the recognition of ethical ideas and the moral strength to put such ideas into daily living," listed only one course on ethics in its undergraduate philosophy department, and no courses at all in its graduate school. Roughly one-fifth of the courses listed in the catalogues would fall into the category of professional ethics. Two-fifths of the surveyed courses as described in the catalogues have ethics as a major theme, and the remainder have ethics as a subtheme. The number of "applied ethics" courses turned out to be about the same as the number of theoretical ethics courses, although the ratio of applied courses to theoretical courses varied considerably from university to university. In general, the large, prestigious universities offer a higher ratio of theoretical to applied courses than do the smaller, less prominent universities. The topical concerns of the applied ethics courses at the latter schools ranged from "secretarial ethics" to "Christian business ethics" to "contemporary newspaper practices."

The professions that seem best represented at both the graduate

---

been a major, and very expensive study in and of itself. Not only did such a study seem well beyond our resources; we were also not convinced that it would have been worth the expenditure of large amounts of time and money even if they had been available. Instead, we worked hard to collect that information already available in scattered books, articles, and unpublished studies and, where possible, to collect some new data when that seemed feasible, useful, and relatively inexpensive. We are confident that we gained enough sample evidence to achieve a sense of the present state of ethics teaching in the United States. We hope that further studies will improve upon our own findings.

and undergraduate level in the applied ethics category are medicine, business, and law; and almost all of the universities surveyed offer a course in "bioethics" or "ethics and the life sciences." Approximately one-quarter of the courses categorized in the survey were taught by the philosophy department, while one-seventh of the total number of courses were taught by the religious studies department; the rest were scattered through almost every department.

A comparative sampling of ethics offerings in philosophy departments from the period 1950–65 revealed very few courses in "applied ethics." Moreover, most of the textbooks and readers used during that period focused very broadly on theoretical questions of ethics. The most important change within the past decade has been an increasing emphasis in textbooks and readers on very concrete issues in ethics: abortion, truth-telling, confidentiality, justice, war and peace, sexual ethics, and the like. No less noteworthy has been the rapid proliferation of courses outside traditional philosophy and religious studies departments, almost all of them with an applied focus. Thus significant content changes are underway in those departments that have traditionally taught ethics, and the introduction of courses in ethics in other departments and divisions of the university is itself a notable phenomenon.

One of the most striking findings of the study was the wide variation in the number of courses offered within different universities in particular states, and in the number of courses offered in universities from state to state. Arkansas, for example, has 20 colleges and universities; among them 28 courses in ethics were offered during the 1977–78 period. In Kansas, by contrast, there are 23 colleges and universities, and 105 courses were offered during that period. At some colleges of comparable size, nearly two or three times as many courses in ethics were offered as in others.

Comparatively speaking, it was much more difficult to assess the state of the teaching of ethics at the undergraduate level, or the prevalence of that teaching, than at the professional school level. No one, so far as we could discover, has attempted a full survey of the teaching of ethics at the undergraduate level, and it was beyond our resources to do so. By contrast, as will be indicated below, a number of studies have been carried out in at least some professional schools and professional areas.

A. Ethics in Undergraduate Education

While we make no claim whatever to scientific completeness, the meetings we held, the correspondence we received, the visits we made, and the consultations we carried out allowed us to come to some tentative general conclusions about the teaching of undergraduate ethics. One of these has already been mentioned: that in traditional departments of philosophy and religion, courses with an emphasis on applied ethics are much more common now than they were a decade ago and seem to be increasing with great rapidity. Beyond that, we had a particular interest in looking at new programs explicitly devoted to ethics, but outside traditional departments altogether, or jointly sponsored by different departments.

While we uncovered a number of exceptions, the following seem to us valid generalizations:

● Most courses and programs outside traditional departments are financed by external short-term grants rather than by general university funds or state appropriations;

● most programs in applied ethics have been initiated within the past ten years;

● most ethics and "values" courses are elective rather than required;

● most such courses are interdisciplinary in content, many are team-taught and not confined to departments of religion or philosophy;

● most use the case-method approach in conjunction with other forms of pedagogy, such as the services of visiting lecturers and continuing seminars;

● most are issue-oriented, e.g., dealing with euthanasia, bribery, atomic power, rather than organized around a very broad ethical theme, e.g., justice, individualism;

● the impetus for the inauguration of special ethics programs comes from many sources, including students, faculty, administration, professional societies;

● an increasing number of courses and programs on ethics are aimed explicitly at preprofessional students;

● ethics programs do not usually constitute student majors but complement them;

• comparatively more ethics courses and programs at the undergraduate level have been instituted at schools that now have, or had, religious or denominational ties than is the case at public institutions;

• some disciplinary friction exists concerning who is qualified to teach ethics and in what manner ethics should be taught;

• many of the new "core curriculum" programs now underway or in the process of development give a prominent place to ethical and "value" issues; yet in few places has that general commitment given rise to systematic programs.

Bernard Murchland has usefully categorized the way ethics is communicated to students in the undergraduate curriculum: (1) through the institution—its structure, its ethos, its traditions, and its particular social status; (2) through the curriculum: the range of course offerings, the comparative emphasis on a broad education or vocationalism, and through the methodologies and other ways of looking at the world that they communicate; (3) through traditional ethics courses or courses in moral reasoning: courses that introduce students to ethical theory, modes of ethical analysis, the history of ethical ideas, and, of late, the application of ethical theory to particular cases; (4) through issue-oriented courses: courses that focus on a range of contemporary debates, whether in the area of bioethics, environmental ethics, or issues such as justice, racism, and sexism; (5) through courses on professional ethics: medical ethics, business ethics, or accounting ethics; (6) through courses on technology and society: courses that examine particular moral problems arising out of technological development, or that look more broadly at the relationship between ethics, technology, and society; (7) through "values clarification"; and (8) through the cognitive moral development movement.[20]

In addition to attempting to gain a broad feel for the teaching of ethics in the undergraduate curriculum, we paid special attention to three areas that have shown special growth in the past few years: science, technology, and ethics; preprofessional ethics; and the introduction of ethical themes and issues into courses in the humanities and the social sciences that are not explicitly listed as courses in ethics.

1. Science, Technology, and Ethics

Perhaps the area of greatest development in recent years has been the proliferation of courses under the general rubric of "science, technology, and human values," and courses in medical ethics or bioethics.[21] While diverse in content, in teaching strategy, and in their general focus, they share an examination of the relationship between science, technology, human values, ethics and the larger society. Two recent studies show that courses in the field of science, technology, and human values (STHV) number over 2,000 and are offered in small colleges, research universities, and in professional schools, with the majority being offered at the undergraduate level.[22] On the whole, STHV courses tend to focus more on the physical sciences and engineering than on the other sciences. When they use the natural sciences as a base for their analysis, they often focus on environmental issues, and on problems of pollution, resource management, agriculture and food production as a major backdrop for an analysis of the societal impact and human implications of scientific and technological developments. Courses on biomedical ethics, by contrast, use the biological and biomedical sciences as their base. About 1,000 such courses are offered each year and probably represent the most common of all courses in the general area of science and ethics.[23]

Under the STHV label, course topics are also likely to include technology assessment, systems analysis, computer technology, energy resources, communications, and cost-benefit analysis. While such courses aim to introduce science and engineering students to a broader view of science and its relationship to other human activities, many such courses are designed for nonscience students as well. Courses in bioethics, aimed at both science and nonscience majors, ordinarily focus on such topics as abortion, genetic counseling and engineering, the causes and treatment of disease, issues concerned with the definition of death and the care of the dying patient, questions of justice and the allocation of medical resources, the use of human beings as research subjects, and the manipulation or control of human behavior by medical or technological means. Materials on aging, population growth, sociobiology, and pollution are also common. On the whole, courses in bioethics offered outside philosophy or religion departments—e.g., in a biology department—tend to be issue- or case-oriented, rather than organized in terms of biological subfields or philosophical theory. By contrast, bioethics courses in philosophy departments tend to be organized around broader philosophical theory, though they make frequent use of cases.

As popular and common as courses in STHV and biomedical ethics are becoming, they present a number of problems. Many of those teaching such courses, or wishing to do so, find themselves inadequately trained, and are often forced to make use of team-teaching, if only because they feel unable to teach the course on their own. (Needless to say, team-teaching can be superb; we are concerned, at this point, only to note that it is sometimes resorted to in order to cope with inadequate teacher training.) Another common problem is that those teaching courses often find it difficult to get a suitable mix between very specific problems and cases, on the one hand, and the introduction to students of broader theory, whether of a scientific or ethical kind, on the other hand. In particular, courses which try to combine both biology and ethics often find themselves stretched thin on both fronts: there is time neither for an adequate introduction to biology as a scientific field, nor to ethics as a proper course of study in itself. At the same time, however, the field of biomedical ethics is now a strong one in terms of scholarly material, anthologies, and other instructional material.[24] That is less the case in the area of science, technology, and human values.

2. Preprofessional Ethics

That courses on professional and preprofessional ethics should be spreading on undergraduate campuses is hardly surprising.[25] The strong trend in higher education in recent years toward a job and career orientation compels those concerned with the teaching of ethics to find ways to integrate ethics into that vocational orientation. Moreover, the widespread criticism and suspicion of many of the professions, their own internal uncertainties, and their prominent role in American life have been the source of considerable interest in problems of professional ethics.

In speaking of professional and preprofessional ethics at the undergraduate level, an important distinction must be kept in mind. Many forms of undergraduate education are themselves essentially professional education. That would be true, for instance, in such fields as engineering, journalism, nursing, accounting, and often enough, business. That graduate programs are also available in those fields should not obscure the fact that much final professional education goes on at the undergraduate level. Thus a large number of the courses in ethics now being introduced at the undergraduate level are attempts to integrate ethics into undergraduate professional education.

Compared with many courses in the area of science, technology, and ethics, or in business ethics, undergraduate courses in professional ethics are focused more on the specific moral dilemmas of professionals than on the broader relationship between the professions and society. Yet the extent to which these courses focus on professional dilemmas—as distinguished from the broader social issues posed by the professions—varies considerably from school to school. Some of this variation seems a function of the perception on the part of professors as to the capacity of students to grapple with larger questions of ethical theory and of the relationship of the professions to society; in part it is due to a strong desire of professors to make ethics appear directly relevant to a professional education, and in part to the relationship of courses in ethics to other courses offered in the professional curriculum.

Given our belief in the value of ethics courses in the undergraduate curriculum, we have every reason to welcome the introduction of such courses into the professional curriculum of those receiving undergraduate degrees. Ideally, they should familiarize students with the kinds of moral problems they will encounter in their professional life or in dealing with professionals, give them some sense of broader moral theory to enable them to relate particular dilemmas to a wider moral outlook and general moral principles, and enable them to get a better understanding of the relationship between their profession and other professions and groups in the society. Many such programs, however, are hampered by the lack of solid scholarly material, by a strong sense on the part of many faculty members of inadequate preparation to teach courses in ethics, and by the difficulty of getting students to take ethics courses as seriously as the more vocation-oriented courses. While the question of the availability of scholarly material and other teaching problems will be discussed further below, there is a general agreement that good undergraduate teaching material has been in short supply in many professional areas, most notably in journalism, nursing, allied health, and business.

A related and important development is the attempt to provide those planning to go on to graduate school in one of the professions with an introduction to problems of professional ethics at the undergraduate level. One purpose of such courses is to enable students to get a better understanding of the professions themselves, not only that they may envision the kind of career they are projecting for themselves, but in some cases that they may judge whether in fact they want to pursue that professional education. Courses in preprofessional ethics are often seen as providing an introduction to the professions themselves, and make use of moral problems in those professions as a way of better understanding the internal dynamics of the profession, as well as its relationship to the broader society. Another and more obvious purpose of such courses is to provide students with an introductory knowledge of the types of ethical issues they are likely to encounter should they continue with their professional plans.

Many who teach such undergraduate courses are convinced that students are not likely to receive a solid introduction to professional ethics in graduate schools. They want to make certain that professional ethics is not neglected altogether. For those who may receive further training in ethics at the professional school level, an undergraduate introduction to the topic will, of course, provide a stronger base for later exposure. Moreover, students may be able to get a different and somewhat broader perspective on the professions at the undergraduate level than is possible once they are immersed in their professional education. They may then approach their careers having at least been exposed to a more critical, detached viewpoint. This aim will be best served if the students in such courses include not only students planning to enter the profession in question, but others as well.

The nature and quality of the schools where courses on ethics are introduced obviously makes a significant difference. Preprofessional ethics courses at smaller liberal arts colleges—where there are smaller classes, more broadly educated students, and faculty drawn heavily from the humanities departments—are in a

much stronger position than schools with a more general technical orientation. Some schools offering undergraduate professional
degrees have exceedingly low humanities requirements, with the
consequence that students come to courses in ethics poorly prepared to grapple with theoretical questions of any kind, to read
difficult material, and to pursue the subject of ethics in a rigorous
way. In such schools, in addition, there are often few faculty
members trained in ethics and it is there particularly that, despite
a high interest, teachers seem to feel the greatest inadequacy
about their capacity to teach the subject. In these schools, too,
fewer resources are available for team-teaching or supplementary
assistance from colleagues.

3. The Teaching of Ethics in Non-ethics Humanities and Social Science Courses

One of the problematic areas in the teaching of ethics is that of
the introduction of ethical themes, issues, and reasoning in
courses that are not explicitly ethics courses at all.[26] Although we
had no way of determining the extent to which this happens, it
became clear to us from many informants, and from our examination of catalogues and course syllabi, that ethical issues are
being introduced into many courses, especially in the humanities
and the social sciences. No one would pretend that a single
course in ethics at the undergraduate level, however solid that
course, could hope to cover the subject fully. Hence, one might
hope that ideally ethical issues would be broached in many other
kinds of courses, at least to some degree. Few areas of human
study or exploration lack ethical dimensions. Courses in literature
can stimulate the moral imagination of students, enable them to
grasp how other lives are lived, and give them a sense of the
profound complexities of the moral life. Courses in history or
politics can show students how moral perspectives and societal
mores have shaped the rise and fall of governments, the development and decline of civilizations. They can shed light, too, on
views that put into question traditional ethical inquiry—the
views, for instance, of Marx or Freud or Sartre. Different forms
of economic systems rest on different moral premises and they
can be explored in an economics course. Examples need not be
multiplied; they are found in every field.

Some caution is nevertheless in order. A major premise of this Report is that ethics is a difficult subject, requires training in its own right, and should be treated with at least the seriousness accorded any other field or discipline. Given that premise, it is important that ethics be introduced in non-ethics courses in a way that does justice to the subject matter. Within departments of philosophy and theology, ethics can be approached with full rigor and be superintended by disciplinary standards and norms. No such protection is guaranteed when scholars or teachers, otherwise untrained in ethics, take up moral issues. It is all too tempting for professors who want to pursue certain ethical issues, or who wish to call attention to certain moral evils they perceive in society, to use non-ethics courses as a vehicle for doing so— and to do so in a context where the students may not be given the appropriate, critical, analytical training necessary to cope with the moral opinions and perspectives urged upon them. While the danger of indoctrination is surely present in formal courses in ethics, it can be far greater in other courses that encompass moral issues.

Our own conclusion represents something of a compromise. We surely would not wish to discourage the introduction of ethical issues in non-ethics courses. That would deprive students of the possibility of recognizing ethical dimensions in other areas of study and work, force professors to leave out important dimensions of their own discipline, and leave the subject of ethics unnecessarily relegated to specific courses. But we would encourage those preparing to give a significant portion of their course over to ethical dilemmas or moral themes to make clear to students their intention to do so. Courses in ethics disguised as courses in literature or history or economics violate both the integrity of ethics as a discipline and the integrity of the other disciplines as well. Yet we foresee that as the teaching of applied ethics spreads, it will be easier for those who take up ethical issues in courses not specifically devoted to ethics to consult with colleagues about course materials and to develop greater familiarity with the field of ethics.[27]

The primary value of introducing ethical themes into non-ethics courses is to awaken students to the broader personal, social, and institutional dimensions of particular fields and disciplines. Such an introduction can serve as a valuable preparation for more systematic modes of ethical thinking. The important point is that the students be led to understand that they are working at an introductory level, that more can and should be done, and that a full pursuit of ethics requires as much seriousness as a full pursuit of the disciplines into which ethics can be introduced.

As the development of courses in the area of science, technology, and human values, in preprofessional programs, and in non-ethics courses in the humanities and social sciences indicates, there are many possible avenues to a confrontation with moral issues. In one sense, it might be said that no one route to an examination of ethics is necessarily better than another. If a course is well-organized and plunges deeply enough, students can readily be exposed to those abiding moral concerns that have marked all thoughtful human life. If contemporary moral questions of scientific research and technology force the asking of some basic questions about the human good and human ends, the same results can be achieved through literature, through an examination of political and social policy, or through a grappling with questions of abortion and prenatal diagnosis. The only slight hazard we would note is that the more specialized routes into ethics may, often of necessity, focus on one range of ethical problems at the expense of others. An undergraduate introduction to ethics which takes place only through a course in bioethics, or the problems of professionals, or the moral dilemmas of social science research, will almost always leave students with less than a complete picture of the full range of ethical theory, moral problems, and human values. Only a combination of courses in ethics and the encountering of moral problems in non-ethics courses is likely to convey that full picture. If a single course is all that is possible, there will be special pressures upon the teachers to use those courses as ways of transcending the particularities of the subject matter to introduce students to a broader range of problems.

We offer some recommendations concerning the teaching of ethics to undergraduates, while recognizing that they may be difficult to achieve in many places. Every undergraduate should have a systematic introduction to both ethical theory and applied ethics. Whether in a single course or, still better, in at least two or more courses, the outcome to be sought is an undergraduate who is alert and sensitive to moral problems, has an understanding of the nature and place of ethical theory, and who has been afforded an opportunity to confront issues in applied ethics in the classroom. Opportunities should exist, moreover, for the more interested student to pursue ethics in advanced courses.

The undergraduate years are an appropriate time for young people to begin fashioning or refining their own moral values and personal moral ideals. Undergraduates need to develop critical skills, not only for an examination of the world and society of which they are a part, but also for that self-examination of personal goals that is a necessary part of individual moral development. At the least, then, undergraduate courses in ethics should aim to contribute directly to student efforts to come to greater self-awareness. Courses should assist students in helping them to frame and understand the kinds of moral problems they will face as individuals and, in the process, assist them in the development of personal moral virtues and ethical ideals. What should we live for? What do we owe to other people? What are the goals of the moral life, and what means are appropriate for achieving them? Those are basic human questions, ones that have confronted all generations; they are central to any reflective human life—and they should be central to any undergraduate curriculum.

The private moral life is always lived in tension—sometimes creative, sometimes not—with the moral lives of others. Hence, in addition to being provided with help in fashioning a personal moral life, students also need help in recognizing and examining the society in which they live, and that society set within the larger context of the human community as a whole. What ought to be the goals of a society, and how should different societies conduct themselves toward each other? What is the nature of a just society, and what is the relationship between human liberty and goals of justice? By what processes, and by whom, should lawmaking be carried on? To what extent should morality be enforced by law? In what circumstances, if any, should laws be protested or even disobeyed? What are the conditions necessary for human community, and how ought the common conflict between individual desires and the common good or public interest be negotiated? The list of questions is long and difficult. The undergraduate years should be an occasion to confront them all, and to begin the process of framing some answers, however rough and approximate.

Neither questions of personal morality nor questions of societal welfare arise in a vacuum. Our personal values will reflect the values of different ethical strands in society and the moral ideals of various ethical theories and perspectives; and the same is true of the values and moralities of societies. A historical and cultural understanding, then, of the origin and history of moral thought is critical. Students should be led to see that others have wrestled with problems they are just discovering, that often, quite unknowingly, what we think unique or special may have a long tradition behind it. Of course this ought to be part of the larger work of the humanities and the liberal arts in general in the undergraduate curriculum. Courses in ethics should by no means have to bear the full burden of exposing students to the history of human values, cultural ideals, and political systems. But courses and programs in ethics should supplement that broader education by a more specific focus on the historical and cultural context of ethical theory and moral reasoning. While it is unlikely that a course or courses in ethics will quickly come to have the central place in the undergraduate curriculum that moral philosophy had in the nineteenth century, those courses can still aspire to an integrative and synthesizing role, one that asks students to work through the deepest of human questions and leaves with them a sense that those questions ought to remain animate with them for the rest of their lives.[28]

B. Ethics in Professional Education

With the exception of courses on science, technology, and human values, and courses on bioethics at the undergraduate level, no change in the teaching of ethics has been so dramatic in recent years as that of the introduction of ethics into professional school curriculums.[29] As noted above, courses on ethics are being rapidly introduced at the undergraduate level for those receiving professional degrees. That development has been stimulated by activities in the graduate and professional schools, and there has been considerable interaction between those two levels. But the phenomenon of a rapid introduction in recent years of courses of ethics into the professional school curriculum is most striking.

A number of reasons suggest themselves for this development: concern for the ethics of professionals, for the role of the professions in society, for the kind of training being provided professionals, and a recognition of the emergence of fresh moral dilemmas within the professions. At the same time, a scholarly interest in the ethical dilemmas of professionals has stimulated a greater interest in the teaching of the subject.

Yet, for all the interest, attempts to give ethics a more central role in the curriculum of professional schools have met with obstacles. They include:

• the dearth of good scholarly literature in some fields;

• a widespread lack of adequate training on the part of many of those who either are teaching courses or would like to do so;

• considerable resistance among other faculty members and administrations to adding one more course into already over-crowded curriculums;

• a lack of funds in many areas to introduce new courses;

• the general ethos of many professional schools, which renders them resistant to subject matter thought by many not to be rigorous, or more appropriate at the undergraduate level, or a distraction from the important business of gaining professional credentials.[30]

We believe that there is as important and significant a place for ethics in professional and graduate curriculums as in the undergraduate curriculum. Ideally, undergraduate programs should have introduced students to ethics so that courses at the professional school level would have a base upon which to build. As a practical matter that is too rarely the case. Hence, courses at the professional school level will ordinarily have to do double duty: provide students with the elements of ethical theory while, at the same time, exposing them to the kinds of moral problems they will encounter as professionals. At present, there are great differences in the extent and quality of ethics teaching from one professional field to another and considerable disagreement on standards of rigor and adequacy for such teaching. Some areas in the teaching of professional ethics are well-developed, whereas others can only be described as rudimentary.

While many of these differences and disparities will be discussed in greater detail below, we will begin with some observations and recommendations.

The most characteristic and common mode for the teaching of ethics in professional schools is that of the case-study method, focusing on particular dilemmas and quandaries and emphasizing the particularities of moral decisionmaking. The advantage of such an approach is that it mirrors the way many other subjects are taught in professional schools, provides students with a feel for the concreteness and particularities of the kinds of problems they will face as professionals, and can readily draw upon material at hand, either in anecdotal or published form. Nonetheless, if not well handled, the case method has limitations. It can convey the sense that all moral issues are discrete, that there are no general features to moral dilemmas, and that there is no room for ethical theory or general principles. All who teach ethics in a professional school confront the problem of a good balance between case material and the introduction of broader theory. Case material is more readily accessible and digestible by students, but an excessive case emphasis can leave students bereft of broader and more general ways of coping with particular dilemmas.

A no less important issue is raised by a general tendency in professional schools to focus on dilemmas faced by individual practitioners. What should I, as a doctor, do with a dying patient? As a journalist, what ought I to do if a court ordered me to give up my notes on a story I wrote? As an engineer, should I blow the whistle when I am faced with flagrant abuse on the part of friends and colleagues? There is a very strong bias toward matters of personal conduct, the resolution of individual dilemmas, and the development of a private morality to cope with personal dilemmas. That is certainly an appropriate focus, but it needs to be supplemented by broader considerations.

We recommend, therefore, that courses in professional ethics at the graduate level include the following emphases: (1) personal ethical dilemmas that will be faced by professionals; (2) the ethical choices and judgments involved in selecting, defining, and analyzing concrete problems, and in weighing, judging, or recommending particular broad policies and patterns of conduct; (3) an analysis of the value dimensions, and implicit biases, of the methodologies and practices of particular disciplines. Students being introduced to ethics at the professional school level should, that is, understand the kinds of personal decisions they are likely to encounter and the broader context of those decisions (where the ethical issues may be as much a matter of policy or institutional practice as of individual dilemmas); and they should recognize that almost all methods or approaches used by particular disciplines in analyzing problems in their field may themselves contain a significant value component.

Beyond those goals, courses in professional ethics should consider the purposes and roles of the particular professions in society; the connection between professionals and employers, clients or patients; the relationship of professionals to colleagues in their own field; the relationship of the profession to the broader society; and the way in which that interaction characteristically takes place.[31] We recognize the difficulty of proposing that teachers of professional ethics attempt to deal with such a broad range of topics and to treat ethics simultaneously at both the personal, the institutional, and the social level. Nonetheless, we believe it useful at least to set forth some ideals for such teaching, recognizing that it must be left to the ingenuity of teachers to find ways, in the context of limited time, to do full justice to the subject.

1. The State of Ethics Teaching in Professional Schools

Any attempt to put together a composite picture of the teaching of ethics in professional schools meets with difficulties.* Al-

---

*Our survey of the teaching of ethics in professional schools, and in particular professional areas, was of necessity selective. We chose to focus our research attention on those areas where some reasonably solid information seemed available or could be developed within our resources, and on those areas that have shown some special activity in recent years. There has, of course, been some activity in almost all professional areas recently, and our research turned up efforts to introduce the teaching of ethics in the fields of accounting, public relations, real estate, and the military, among others. Other major and traditional professions, such as the ministry, the academic profession, and architecture would each be worth studies in their own right, but were ones that we could not undertake.

though the available data on the number and extent of courses in ethics is far stronger at the professional than at the undergraduate level, there are nonetheless many gaps in that data. It is often difficult to determine the background or original discipline of those teaching the courses, the extent to which their teaching of ethics represents a major scholarly or pedagogical interest (or is secondary only), and the extent to which the available courses are warmly or coolly received, both in terms of the quality of the teaching and in terms of the status they have in the curriculum. Nonetheless, we offer the following generalizations based on our study of seven areas of professional education: law, business, public policy, biomedicine, journalism, engineering, and the social sciences. Additional data was also available on nursing and allied health fields.

Little sense can be made of the teaching of professional ethics without understanding the character of professional schools. With the exception of graduate schools in the social sciences, their primary purpose is to provide students with those specialized skills, bodies of knowledge, and attitudes needed for them to work as professionals in society. Both the faculty and administrations assume that their students have already had a general education, that professional schools neither are nor should be equipped to remedy deficiencies in that general education, and that the ultimate test of the value of the education is technical competence. This is not to deny that there are many experiments and curriculum reforms at present underway in professional education. Some professional schools are more oriented toward broader social and political issues than others, and toward introducing their students to considerations which go beyond competence only. Many individual faculty members will have both scholarly and pedagogical interests that are broader than the merely technical. Still, professional education is strongly job- and profession-oriented: it transmits specific skills. That is what students expect when they enroll in such schools, what professors are trained and prepared to give them, and what employers who are going to hire the graduates look for.

Given that context, the introduction of courses in ethics is rarely greeted with general enthusiasm, and their role in programs oriented in very different directions is uneasy. Yet the difficulties go beyond ethics teaching. It is striking how few professional schools offer students an opportunity to examine the nature of their profession—its historical roots, its function in society, its sociological characteristics, and its assumptions about the political and social order.[32] Such questions will of course arise during a professional education, but few professional schools seem to think it valuable to confront them in any systematic fashion. If that is the case even with the professions themselves, it is easy to understand why courses in professional ethics, which inevitably involve the nature of the professions in question, find they must operate in an atmosphere that is cool at best and at times positively hostile.

With the exception of medicine and law, it is difficult in any of the professional school areas to find more than a handful of faculty members for whom ethics (or "professional responsibility," as it is often called) is a major academic and teaching interest. It is equally rare to discover schools where courses on ethics have a central role in the curriculum—the overwhelming majority are elective courses, for instance. With only two exceptions that we could discern, scholarly work in ethics will not routinely assist younger faculty members in gaining tenure within traditional specialized departments. One of those exceptions is in the law, where if scholarship in law and professional responsibility is not strongly encouraged, it is nonetheless seen as a substantive area. The other exception, just beginning to appear, would be in those few professional schools that go out of their way to hire people to teach ethics, making it clear at the outset that their scholarship in the field of ethics will be judged by the criteria appropriate to that field. This is happening in some medical and engineering schools, but remains rare in other schools.

In essence, then, the teaching of ethics in almost all professional schools can be characterized as follows: it is seen as at best a secondary or tertiary function of the schools; those who teach such courses are likely to be seen either as outside, or only barely on the fringe of, the main purposes of the schools; and those attempting to introduce ethics courses can normally expect considerable disinterest or resistance. Finally, the curriculum of almost all professional schools is already overcrowded, many are beginning to experience financial strain, and the schools are already subject to pressure either to increase the time given to subjects already in the curriculum or to add still others of a technical nature.[33] Given these realities, the teaching of ethics is hardly the most prominent feature of professional education in the United States. At the same time, the current lack of attention to ethics in many professional schools is a source of considerable professional uneasiness, especially because professional schools have always claimed to take the moral role of professionals seriously.

2. A Profile of the Teaching of Professional Ethics

All professions, nevertheless, show a new interest in the teaching of ethics, and experience some degree of both external and internal pressures to introduce such courses. One helpful way of looking at the present status of the teaching of professional ethics is to begin with those professional fields where the teaching of ethics is fairly well advanced.

Among the strongest is that of medical ethics. Surveys undertaken in 1972 and 1974 revealed a significant growth and institutionalization of medical ethics teaching in medical schools.[34] Out of 110 medical schools in the United States, about 90 percent now offer at least some exposure to the subject. In the 1974 survey, 53 schools reported having faculty members with some specific responsibility in the area of medical ethics, and 31 faculty members were identified for whom the teaching of medical ethics was one of their primary tasks (e.g., one to which they devoted at last half of their time). Although about half of the medical schools in this country still offer very little in the way of systematic training in ethics, practically all schools now feel the need to have at least some course, or subsection of a course, devoted to the subject. While there is still a tendency in medical schools to assign the teaching of ethics to those trained in medicine only, or occasionally in one of the social sciences, a number of medical schools in recent years have added philosophers or theologians to their faculties to teach ethics.

Most important, perhaps, the field of medical ethics, or bioethics, has become a major area of scholarly interest, drawing upon those primarily trained in ethics, but increasingly attracting those with medical or science degrees as well. A few universities are beginning to offer specialized graduate programs in the area,[35] numerous summer workshops and intensive programs are offered in the field,[36] and the many undergraduate courses in bioethics have stimulated students to request still more while in medical school. That so many of the moral dilemmas of contemporary biomedical research and clinical practice have received widespread exposure in the media—the Karen Ann Quinlan case, recombinant DNA research, the widespread introduction of prenatal diagnosis, psychosurgery—has given the status of ethical issues in medicine a dramatic focus unmatched by most other fields.

The fresh interest in ethics in graduate philosophy programs and in religious studies programs (not to mention the critical shortage of traditional humanities teaching jobs) has drawn many to medical ethics in recent years. They are beginning to provide a reservoir upon which medical schools can and do draw. The development in a few schools of broad programs on the humanities and medicine—encompassing literature, history, some of the social sciences, political science, and economics—has given ethics a broader context than that of a single course or program in medical ethics alone. National debate over the quality and cost of medical care, the goals of health-care delivery, widespread concern about an excessive emphasis on technology in medicine, and the desire to train more physicians who will go into family or general practice, all have stimulated a greater willingness to consider questions of ethics. If the teaching of ethics in medical schools still has a considerable distance to go, it is the one area we examined where there now exists some agreement upon methods for teaching ethics, and upon qualifications needed for the teaching of ethics; the one area, too, where solid and varied materials are available for use in the classrooms—textbooks, case books, and collected readings.

Many American law schools have traditionally offered and required of their students a separate course on legal ethics or professional responsibility.[37] Since 1974, the American Bar Association has mandated, through accreditation standards, that schools teach the "history, goals, structure, and responsibilities of the legal profession and its members, including the ABA Code of Professional Responsibility."[38]

While these traditions and new developments might suggest considerable strength in the field, the reality is less vigorous. One recent study showed that 133 of the 156 accredited law schools require completion of a course in professional responsibility.[39] Yet one-third of those courses comprise only about 15 hours of instruction, one-half of the minimum standard one-term law school course. A survey of over 1,300 law students from seven law schools disclosed that the ethics course has unusually low status in the curriculum hierarchy: it is perceived by students to be less valuable, to require less time and effort, and to be more poorly taught than other law school courses.[40] Comparatively speaking, the field still lacks sophisticated writing in the area of law, ethics, and professional responsibility, particularly in relationship to what is available for other law school courses. Relatively few professors in law schools consider legal ethics their primary scholarly interest. Nevertheless, a new journal has been created—*The Journal of the Legal Profession*—and over ten new textbooks as well as a considerable body of scholarly articles have appeared in the past few years.[41] There is every indication that a more theoretical and systematic examination of the legal profession and its responsibilities is under way.

A somewhat different situation exists in schools of business.[42] Despite numerous recent discussions and conferences on ethics and business, the creation of special groups and centers to deal with the teaching of ethics in business schools, and a number of recommendations by professional groups that ethics be treated more systematically in the curriculum, the academic response has been meager. Most business schools do not have separate courses in business ethics, few include it as a required course, and few have faculty members who have teaching of ethics as a primary responsibility. The field of business ethics still lacks a coherent and scholarly body of literature, and is exceedingly short on people with experience and training in both ethics and business management.

The belief that business education should include the social dimensions of corporate conduct has been commonplace among those responsible for shaping the focus of business school curriculums for the last twenty years. More recently, the business school profession itself began to stress the importance of including course work on the environment of business. Nonetheless, despite this emphasis—construed to include ethical considerations—there are comparatively few courses that focus exclusively on business ethics. On the whole, ethics is most likely to be part of other courses, with little indication at present that separate courses on business ethics will be widely introduced. Few schools have hired someone with training in philosophical or theological ethics; and where that has happened, those teaching have rarely had any formal training in business or economics. Those with such training who do teach business ethics have seldom had any training in ethics. In general there is a dearth of persons sufficiently experienced in both ethics and business management theory or practice to warrant full faculty status. Nonetheless, because of both internal and external pressures, interest in the subject is rising.

A still different situation can be found in graduate schools of social sciences.[43] During the past decade there has been considerable discussion of the ethics of social science research. It has turned on such issues as the deception of subjects in social psychology experiments, the uses and abuses of surveys and opinion polls, moral problems posed by contract research, the legitimacy of crossnational studies such as Project Camelot, and the relationship of social research to policymaking. Books have been published on these subjects, conferences run, and symposia organized. As a result of federal regulations, social science research involving human beings is now subject to the approval of Institutional Review Boards (IRBs), and thus the subject of considerable debate. In spite of these developments, only a handful of courses are devoted wholly or substantially to ethics in the social sciences.

The attitude toward the teaching of ethics in anthropology, psychology, and sociology has shifted in recent years from outright hostility to wariness and skepticism. Some say that the teaching of ethics is basically irrelevant, that the ethical issues raised by the social sciences are too trivial to deserve scarce class time. Others regard the teaching of ethics as part of the larger assault on research freedom personified by Institutional Review Boards. A few are worried that ethics has become an outlet for ideological indoctrination. Still, the teaching of ethics in the social sciences is on the upswing, particularly in the form of lectures and readings in other courses. Discussions of ethics now make their way with increasing frequency into courses bearing other titles, especially on research methods, and other signs indicate that ethics is becoming an acceptable topic of discussion in these disciplines. Our study identified about one hundred social scientists with some professional interest in ethics, even though very few consider it a major area of teaching, research, or writing. There is not a great deal of material available for class-room use, and the existing literature is especially weak on philo-sophical analysis as distinct from issue-raising. Still, all signs suggest that there will be more activity in this area over the coming decade, though it is doubtful that the more positivistically oriented social scientists will ever be warm to this line of teach-ing.[44] Yet, to judge from work now in process, the prospects for an effective blending of disciplinary self-reflection with careful ethical analysis are improving. We predict that the climate for the teaching of ethics in the social sciences will gradually shift from wariness to tolerance, with occasional pockets of enthusiasm.

Schools of nursing show a considerable interest in the teaching of ethics, with little of the ambivalence encountered in the social sciences.[45] They show neither hostility nor indifference to the subject. Many of those teaching nursing ethics are working hard to strengthen the courses, to improve their own background in the subject, and to develop a scholarly literature in the field. None-theless, for all of the enthusiasm, the literature on the subject is only beginning to develop. No published collections of cases exist, nor are there sophisticated collections of readings in the field. In particular, those teaching nursing ethics frequently com-plain that they are forced to turn to the broader literature of medical ethics, much of which focuses on the ethical dilemmas of physicians, ordinarily very different in character than those confronted by nurses. As a result of a widespread movement on the part of nurses to see their profession accorded a higher social and professional status, and because of the desire for classroom material directed specifically to the problems of nurses, considerable interest has been shown in developing an adequate literature. With one exception, that literature has not appeared.[46]

As different as the two professions are, nursing shares one important characteristic with the field of engineering. A number of recent conferences, grants, and fellowship programs have sought to provide training for those in each of the two fields to develop a more solid background for the teaching of ethics. The Kennedy Foundation has supported a fellowship program on nursing ethics, specifically designed to help develop a more scholarly literature and better teaching. Rensselaer Polytechnic Institute was recently awarded a large grant from the National Endowment for the Humanities to assist in the training of more teachers in the field of engineering ethics, and for the development of case and other studies of ethics and engineering.

But despite the rapid proliferation of courses on technology and society in schools of engineering, relatively little has been done specifically in the area of engineering ethics at either the undergraduate or graduate level.[47] Many ethical problems associated with the engineering profession have never been explicitly recognized or discussed to any significant degree outside the profession. The few exceptions have focused on widely publicized events, such as the Goodrich "aircraft brake scandal" and the Bay Area Rapid Transit (BART) engineers' case. There are probably no more than twenty schools of engineering in the country (out of a total of more than 250) that have courses specifically and entirely devoted to the topic of engineering ethics. Such courses are not required; they normally attract small enrollments. In this field, as in others such as nursing, journalism, and the social sciences, there is a striking lack of scholarly books devoted to the subject, of readers for classroom use, and of collected case studies.[48] The call of a number of professional engineering societies for an increased consideration of ethical issues in the curriculum, particularly the undergraduate engineering curriculum, gives reason to believe, however, that courses will increase in the near future and that they will influence graduate education as well.

A slightly different pattern is again manifested in schools of journalism, media, and communications.[49] Questions of media ethics have received considerable public attention of late. Important Supreme Court decisions have turned on the rights and privileges of journalists, and those who work in the media face a wide range of ethical issues. In a general sense journalism schools have included courses in professional ethics within their curriculums since the twenties, although in some schools such courses broadened their focus in the forties and fifties into considerations of "professional responsibility" or of the relationship of media generally with the larger society. Ethical issues are addressed not only in formal courses, but are discussed as well in the relevant context of other instruction in a majority of schools. Yet when one looks for specific courses with the word "ethics" included in the titles, no more than a quarter of schools of media or communication make such offerings. Those teaching the ethics courses usually have a background of professional experience, with formal training in law or history more probable than in ethics. The number of available books on journalism ethics have been until recently comparatively few; most are short on ethical theory, and solid casebooks are only beginning to appear.[50] A number of older books on journalism ethics are being revised. Interest in the field is quickening, however; the subject has been a focus of interest at national meetings of journalism educators in the last few years, ethics requirements are being tightened in accrediting standards for schools generally, and several conferences focusing on ethics are now in the planning stages.

A noteworthy feature of most of the available literature on journalism ethics is that it is almost totally devoid of references to contemporary work in the fields of philosophical or theological ethics. In that respect, an analogous situation was found in some of the other professional fields we studied: a reasonably large body of literature on ethical and value questions, but a literature that makes little or no use of work done within the field of ethics itself. This is particularly true in the area of science and human values literature, in the literature of business ethics, and as mentioned, the literature of journalistic ethics.

The teaching of ethics in schools of public policy and of public administration varies significantly from school to school.[51] At some schools a fairly important role is given to courses in ethics. In others, comparatively little interest is shown and no opportunities for systematic ethical inquiry are provided. Is there any common denominator in these variations? Schools with strong political science components and a pervasive interest in broad questions of public policy and society are much more likely to take seriously ethics courses than schools more heavily oriented toward economics, and toward a heavy emphasis on the teaching of such technical skills as the use of computers, cost-benefit analysis, microeconomics and systems analysis. Schools with a heavy orientation toward quantification, decision theory, and other techniques designed to facilitate "rational" decisionmaking often look upon ethics as "soft" and "subjective." Some see ethics as at most irrelevant, and at worst likely to interfere with the technical education of students. In this field, there exist no casebooks on ethics, few scholarly books given over to the ethical issues of policy analysis, and only a relatively small supply of solid articles for classroom use. Yet the available literature and course syllabi do show a stronger component of ethical theory than is the case in many other fields (e.g., nursing and journalism).[52]

A number of faculty members in schools of public policy are working hard to see ethics given a stronger role in the curriculum. That most of them come from the field of political science, rather than the field of economics, reflects a tension between those two disciplines in the schools. No comparable tension was discovered in the other professional schools that we studied (though in medical and engineering schools the teaching of ethics is frequently associated with the humanities or the social sciences, and thus is well down on the list of those fields and disciplines that have prestige within those schools).

Despite what may appear a rather dismal picture of the actual teaching of ethics in almost all professional schools, every one of the disciplines possesses a core of teachers and scholars and a body of administrators determined both to improve the scholarship in the area of ethics and to find a more important role for ethics within the curriculum. That some professional organizations and societies have issued calls for a stronger role for the teaching of ethics—the American Association of Medical Colleges, the American Bar Association, the American Council for Education in Journalism, and the National Society of Professional Engineers, for example—points to external pressures from the professions themselves to advance the teaching of ethics. The climate for such teaching is changing rapidly, and ethics seems almost certain to play a more prominent role in professional education in the future.

III. Major Issues in the Teaching of Ethics

The teaching of ethics is not likely to flourish in American higher education, or sustain itself as a legitimate and necessary subject, unless there is at least some agreement on the very nature of the enterprise and on appropriate standards of quality and competence. A number of confusions, uncertainties, and differences exist, and it is the purpose of this section to set forth our conclusions concerning the most important of them.

A. Goals in the Teaching of Ethics

The two most frequently voiced sources of confusion and uncertainty about the teaching of ethics concern the nature of its goals and the relationship between the teaching of ethics and the development of moral character and behavior. While the two subjects overlap considerably, the question of goals in the teaching of ethics will be considered first.

One source of uncertainty is that the motives for introducing courses are often very different, thus creating questions about just which goals or purposes are appropriate in which teaching contexts. In some professional schools, for instance, the main motive seems to have been some external pressure, particularly pressure to introduce ethics in order that graduates might *behave* better in their professional lives. In other professional schools, the essential motive is that of grappling with some very specific moral issues in the professional field (e.g., privacy versus the public's right to information), in order to see if some of them can be resolved. In still other schools, the main motive is simply that of introducing different disciplinary and methodological perspectives into professional schools dominated by heavy technical and vocational components. The motives for introducing ethics courses into the undergraduate curriculum are no less varied: "sensitizing" students, teaching them intellectual skills, and helping them with personal problems. Thus many individuals look to courses in ethics to serve different functions, ranging from character improvement, to the development of skills in problem resolution, to a desire simply to expand student horizons, through a desire to satisfy external critics.

Our own general conclusion can be stated quite directly. We believe that the primary purpose of courses in ethics ought to be to provide students with those concepts and analytical skills that will enable them to grapple with broad ethical theory in attempting to resolve both personal and professional dilemmas, as well as to reflect on the moral issues facing the larger society.

All courses in ethics, whether at the undergraduate or professional level, should seek to fulfill a number of highly important goals, goals so central as ordinarily to be indispensable.[53]

1. Stimulating the Moral Imagination

A course in ethics is but an abstract intellectual exercise unless the students' feelings and imagination are stimulated. Students should be encouraged to understand that there is a "moral point of view" (to use Kurt Baier's phrase),[54] that human beings live their lives in a web of moral relationships, that a consequence of moral positions and rules can be actual suffering or happiness, and that moral conflicts are frequently inevitable and difficult. The ability to gain a feel for the lives of others, some sense of the emotions and the feelings that are provoked by difficult ethical choices, and some insight into how moral viewpoints influence the way individuals live their lives would be important outcomes of attempts to stimulate the moral imagination.

The emotional side of students must be elicited or evoked— empathy, feeling, caring, sensibility. Even here, though, the cognitive must quickly enter: to discern hidden assumptions, to notice consequences of thought and behavior, to see that pain and pleasure do not merely happen. The use of novels, plays, and films, or the personal experience of students, can be very effective for this purpose, often far more successfully stimulating the imagination than can ordinary reading fare in philosophical or theological ethics. Care must be taken here, however: courses that depend almost exclusively on visual or fictional material can swamp the imagination while starving the mind. Our feelings of sorrow, pity, anguish, or outrage may be delivering true messages. But that can never be taken utterly for granted, and the minimal perception to be conveyed to students is the possible difference between what they feel at first to be right or good and what they later conclude.

2. Recognizing Ethical Issues

A very fine line separates a stimulation of the moral imagination and a recognition of ethical issues. It is precisely at that point where the classroom emphasis should shift from the emotions and feelings that have been evoked to a conscious, rational attempt to sort out those elements in emotional responses that represent appraisal and judgment, however inchoate at first. How should one characterize and rationally articulate a felt response of injustice, or the violation of a person's autonomy, or the nature of the anguish felt in the face of a decision about whether to keep a severely defective child alive?

Beyond an appraisal of emotional responses, courses should emphasize that many technical, social, psychological, and political problems raise fundamental questions of right and wrong, good and bad. A course in ethics should strengthen an ability to detect hidden value biases and tacit moral premises and to discern when and how issues of morality are present—human rights, for instance, or conflicting moral obligations. A capacity to sift out ethical issues and to see the moral implications of individual and collective decisions are all-important teaching goals.

3. Developing Analytical Skills

Part of the process of recognizing moral issues will require an examination of concepts—of "justice," "autonomy," "dignity," "rights"; of prescriptive moral statements—"defective children should (or should not) be allowed to die"; and of ethical principles and moral rules. Those are the tools of rationality in ethics, the means by which some order is given to the relatively untutored deliverances of experience and previous conditioning.

If concepts, rules, and principles are the tools of rationality in ethics, then skills must be developed to use them. The definition of concepts, the import and consequence of moral rules, and the meaning and scope of general ethical principles will all have to be explored. Concepts such as "justice," "right," and "good," are all disputed and complex notions. There exists a literature on those concepts, broad schools of thought and a history to which students can normally be introduced relatively quickly.

Coherence and consistency are minimal goals for the development of analytical skills, both in the analysis of ethical propositions and of moral actions and in the justification of rules, principles, and specific moral decisions. Ethical principles and moral rules have implications both of a logical and practical kind. Ways must be found to trace out those implications, an exercise requiring both reason and imagination. A moral choice will have consequences, for the individual making the choice and for those affected by it. That needs to be pointed out, if it is not immediately obvious. But are the *consequences* of moral choice and action the only pertinent criteria in judging their validity? Or are there some moral principles so central and so critical to a decent human life that they must be embraced regardless of the consequences? Must actions be right to be moral, or are good intentions enough? These are very old questions, but ones with which every student of ethics will have to wrestle. Just how deeply a teacher should attempt to press such questions, or to emphasize analytical skills, will usually be a matter of prudential judgment on the part of the teacher, based on student capacity and previous preparation. But since such skills are a fundamental part of the very enterprise of ethics, they cannot be left out of even the most basic introductory course.

4. Eliciting a Sense of Moral Obligation and Personal Responsibility

"Why ought I to be moral?" That is a fundamental question in ethics, and a topic to which students should be rapidly introduced. It is an old and exceedingly complex question. What does it mean to take ethics seriously? Does it simply mean recognizing the logical implications of certain moral rules or behavior, or is there a stronger entailment: that one ought necessarily to do that which one perceives to be good or right? There are no easy answers to those questions, and students will have to wrestle with them just as did previous generations. Any course on ethics must explore the role, in practice, of freedom and personal responsibility. It makes no sense to talk of ethics unless one presupposes that individuals have some freedom to make moral choices and that they are responsible for the choices they make.

5. Tolerating—and Resisting—Disagreement and Ambiguity

Students need to learn to tolerate the disagreements and to be prepared to accept the inevitable ambiguities in attempting to examine ethical problems. We can and do differ with our closest friends on matters of ethics, and many ethical issues admit of no final, clear resolution. At the same time, while there must be toleration of disagreement and ambiguity, there must no less be an attempt to locate and clarify the sources of disagreement, to resolve ambiguity so far as possible, and to see if ways can be found to overcome differences of moral viewpoint and theory. Progress can be made in reducing disagreement, in more precisely sorting out elements of ethical disagreement, and thus in gaining a narrower, and perhaps more manageable, area of disagreement—and resolution of disagreement is sometimes possible.

In the teaching of ethics, as in the teaching of every subject, an important purpose should be that of providing students with an introduction to those concepts and analytical skills that will enable them to finally dispense with the need for a teacher, and thus to be able to handle moral issues on their own. Bernard Rosen has articulated that goal well: "One desirable result of education, whatever the area and whatever the subject, is the dispensability of the teacher."[55]

We do not want to imply here that all moral judgments are idiosyncratic, though it is obviously true that our final, personal moral judgments will and must be individual judgments, the consequences of which will be our personal responsibility. Yet we do gain our ethical concepts from the society in which we live, the moral options open to us are finite, and it is as wise in this area as in any other to consult the moral views and reasoning of others before reaching personal judgments.

Our list of important goals in the teaching of ethics points in one general direction: that having elicited the feelings and emotions of students, a very rapid movement must be made into the full rigor of the subject. Students should be led to understand that there are general standards by which to judge the quality of ethical arguments, that disagreements are inevitable but can be reduced, that personal rancor is out of place in the classroom, and that a course on ethics, even at an advanced level, will inevitably leave many problems unexplored and many questions unanswered.

Yet, if some goals are important in all courses, certain specific ethical topics will be more appropriate in some courses than in others. Topics that might be suitable in general introductory courses for undergraduates might be considerably less so in a course on professional responsibility in a law school or when grappling with moral problems of corporate decisionmaking in a business school. The following list will suggest contexts in which different topics might be examined.

1. *Advanced ethical inquiry.* All courses, even the most introductory, should expose students to the existence of advanced ethical inquiry and ethical theory. Advanced courses should simply continue and develop in an increasingly more sophisticated way issues and problems touched upon in introductory courses. Advanced ethical theory should include:

a. An understanding of, and ability to analyze, ethical concepts in their full complexity (e.g., rights, justice, liberty, virtue, autonomy).
b. Familiarity with the history of the development of ethical theories and with the critique to which those theories have been subjected (e.g., utilitarianism and the objections leveled against it).
c. Familiarity with metaethical issues (e.g., the justification of moral judgments).

2. *The social and psychological setting of ethical systems and moral behavior.* The findings and perspectives of disciplines out-

side philosophy and theology can be illuminating to ethical inquiry. Ethical theories do not arise in a cultural vacuum, moral rules are normally fashioned to meet particular political and social needs, and moral judgments are made by human beings with both rational minds and emotional responses. Familiarity with social and psychological contexts would include:

   a. An understanding of the general cultural, social, and political contexts that can lead to, and sustain, particular ethical theories and modes of ethical reasoning; and which will help to explain concepts such as equality and freedom, as well as the particular moral rules, mores, and practices of a given historical period or culture.

   b. Familiarity with the general theories and findings of moral psychology.

   c. Familiarity with those aspects of sociology and anthropology concerned with the development of ethical and value systems and practices.

3. Elements of applied ethics. This category of topics would include those elements necessary to wrestle effectively with problems of normative decisionmaking. Particularly in a professional context, but often as well in a personal context, normative decisionmaking—the domain of "applied ethics"—will involve an understanding of the relationship between ethical theory, moral rules, and the particular scientific, social, or other facts that combine to give a particular decision its specificity and concreteness.

   a. *General*

     (1) A detailed understanding of the official codes, and unofficial mores, of whatever discipline or profession is the subject of a course (e.g., the code of Hippocrates for medical students, or the Code of Professional Responsibility of the American Bar Association for law students or for students taking preprofessional courses in law and ethics).

     (2) A general understanding of the historical origin and the social significance of the pertinent professional code or codes; and a critical awareness of the objections leveled against the codes, both from within a profession and from the outside.

     (3) An understanding of any contrast between provisions of the code (or accepted mores) and the more general morality of the society; and a capacity to analyze the provisions of the code both from the perspective of the profession and the perspective of the broader society.

   b. *Specific*

     (1) An understanding of pertinent factual components that need to be considered in professional decisionmaking (e.g., medical and biological data pertinent to bioethical decisions, or economic and social science

data pertinent to ethical issues of public policy).

(2) An understanding of the explicit or implicit value or ethical premises of the characteristic methodologies employed by particular disciplines and professions (e.g., the value assumptions of cost-benefit analysis in public policy, or the use of deception in some forms of social psychology research).

(3) An understanding of the characteristic ethical problems that face particular professions or disciplines (e.g., informed consent in medical and social science research; conflict of interest in law, business, and accounting; cost-benefit analysis in medicine and engineering; privacy and confidentiality in law, medicine, and journalism; the political uses and abuses of research findings in the social and policy sciences).

One goal frequently proposed for courses in ethics is missing from our list: that of changing student behavior. It was the most troublesome issue we had to face. Many educators and others, we discovered, believe there is no point in teaching an ethics course unless it will assure improvement in student conduct. We have concluded that this is not an appropriate explicit goal for a course in ethics. At the least, it would be naive to pin one's hope for improvement in behavior on any course. Moreover, to bring about such changes, professors might engage in highly questionable techniques of manipulation. These would not only be inappropriate; they would also beg some important moral questions— about what constitutes improvement, for instance—that are precisely those that students should be free to debate.

Having raised those objections, however, it may be possible to specify at least one sense in which courses on ethics could set the stage for behavioral change. They should, at a minimum, provide students with the skills necessary to change their verbal behavior, i.e., by providing them with the tools for a more articulate and consistent means of justifying their moral judgments and of describing the process of their ethical thinking. To be sure, the verbal behavior may represent nothing more than clever sophistry; bad moral positions can be skillfully defended. That danger must be run in order that students learn the necessity of providing public and articulated reasons for their ethical conclusions.

With respect to behavior, however, the most important goal would be that of providing the student with those ingredients of ethical analysis and self-criticism such that a student would, *if* the analysis seemed to require it, recognize the importance of changing behavior and be prepared to change. The question is not whether courses should automatically change behavior, but whether the course would help a student to know the importance of changing his or her behavior, if that was what a moral judgment seemed to entail. It is not change *per se* that should be the goal, but the potential for change as a result of ethical analysis and judgment.

No one wishes to exclude the possibility of changes in conduct as a result of courses in applied ethics. Encouraging students to perceive moral issues more acutely and to reason them out more carefully may well provide a focus for exploring personal changes. It is the emphasis on predetermined moral conclusions that must be avoided. And the courses will have served an important purpose so long as they help students perceive, articulate, and analyze moral problems, even in the absence of direct effects on conduct.

B. Indoctrination and Pluralism

At the heart of much of the ambivalence about the teaching of ethics is a pervasive worry that such courses will become occasions for indoctrination.[56] Closely related to that concern is a no less fundamental uncertainty about whether courses in ethics should be taught in a pluralistic society. If ours is a pluralistic society, espousing no "official" morality, would not ethics courses tend to impose or insinuate a particular set of values or moral principles, thus endangering pluralism?

The concept of "pluralism" itself is something of a puzzle and, as with many other basic concepts, subject to different interpretations and theories. "Pluralism" may, in one sense, simply be a descriptive thesis—that we live in a society marked by the wide range of moral and political values, values that are often in conflict. "Pluralism" can also be understood as a normative doctrine, expressing a positive commitment to the preservation of diverse values and the facilitation of individual freedom. Whatever the particular concept, however, we live in a society where toleration is, at least in principle, highly valued. We are expected to accept the fact that others have different values, come to different moral judgments, and live their lives in the light of different ethical theories. For some, recognition of the mere fact of ethical pluralism carries with it an obligation to be tolerant of a variety of moral viewpoints. The obligation of tolerance embodies, further, a subsidiary duty to refrain from doing that which might undermine the existing plurality of values. Given these widely shared values, the concern that the teaching of ethics not endanger the pluralistic fabric of our society is understandable.

A stronger objection to the teaching of ethics is voiced by those who espouse a normative doctrine of pluralism. To hold that ethical pluralism is a correct way of ordering society is to be committed to allowing diverse value positions to play themselves out in the social and political processes of society. The natural interplay of these value forces is, therefore, likely to be thwarted by a conscious effort to examine and possibly criticize them in the classroom. A closely related concern is voiced by others. Students who come to universities with deeply rooted religious or ethical values, or strong traditions of ethnic or other values, may have their convictions and commitments undermined by classes in ethics—their particular values will not necessarily be cherished or advanced. That concern may be seen as simply another way of defending a form of normative pluralism: students have a right to hold on to and to develop the particular traditions and value systems out of which they come. It would thus, so the objection goes, be wrong for those values to be directly examined.

We do not believe that the teaching of ethics—if carefully defined and delineated—and a normative or descriptive doctrine of pluralism need be incompatible. First, the goals we have proposed above for the teaching of ethics do not entail any conclusion that the details of some moral systems, ethical theories, or moral rules are more correct than others. Those goals point in the direction of the development of a greater understanding of ethical principles and of the skills necessary to analyze such principles. The history of Western philosophical thought— not to mention the more pedestrian experience of classrooms— indicates that those who hone such skills can and do come out with different moral judgments.

Second, we would note that it is a widely stated purpose of a higher education to lead students to greater critical inquiry and

self-awareness. With the exception, perhaps, of some denominational schools, the broad premise of American higher education is
that students must begin at that stage in life to establish their own
world views and independent judgments, and to be prepared to
move in whatever direction seems to them correct.

Third, while it is frequently a feature of classes on ethics that
hard cases and difficult decisions are analyzed, it would be a
serious mistake to underestimate the extent of cultural agreement
on a number of important moral rules and of acceptable behavior.
It is considered wrong to murder, to lie, to steal, to break
promises, to manipulate others for personal gain, and to violate
the dignity and bodies of others. For all of the diversity of
religious and other ethical traditions, they all share an agreement,
in general outline, on those principles.[57] They are the basis of our
legal system and of our normal standards of day-to-day conduct.

The ethical problems that arise concerning that shared agreement normally come at a variety of critical junctures: when it is
necessary to spell out exactly what is meant by accepted principles; when principles come into conflict with each other (the
perennial tension, for example, between a commitment to freedom and a commitment to justice); and when it is necessary to
determine how even widely accepted general principles ought to
be brought to bear on complicated, particular issues. The examination of such difficulties and dilemmas ought to be at the core
of any solid course on ethics. They can ordinarily be explored
without subverting the general moral rules of our culture. To be
sure, the various religious and philosophical traditions ground
these general moral rules in very different ways. How they are
best to be justified is itself an often far more difficult problem
than simply agreeing, in practice, to accept those rules. There
always has and always will be a tension between even the most
solidly grounded moral beliefs and the realities of daily life,
which constantly press intellectual, personal, and social challenges. A major purpose of a course in ethics is to work through
those challenges. The university potentially provides one of the
best arenas in our society for doing just that, and quite apart from
the personal value for students of ethics courses, the latter can
provide a formal forum within the university to grapple with
inescapable issues of human life.

In stressing that courses on ethics need not, and ordinarily will not, serve to erode some well-established traditional values, we do not want to deny the legitimacy of a careful analysis of those values. They ought not to be accepted passively or uncritically. Each generation of students must appropriate them anew. That can only be done if students are willing and able to question their permanent validity, to treat them temporarily with some skepticism, and to bring them to the test of searching inquiry.

Yet, if it can be agreed that the teaching of ethics poses no threat *in principle* to pluralism, is there not reason for a much more precise concern: that individual teachers of ethics will use the classroom as forums for indoctrination of students into the values of the professor? That is surely a possibility, and no doubt in some places a reality. Whether in ethics or other classes, many, if not most, teachers will have their own moral convictions, sometimes strong and obvious, sometimes subtle or not immediately detectable. And if it is perfectly understandable and acceptable that teachers of ethics (like any other human beings) will and should have moral convictions, can one reasonably expect those convictions to be totally suppressed in the classroom? Would that not in itself be a form of moral abdication? But if they are not suppressed, and are allowed clear expression, does that not then raise the specter of indoctrination?

While we have encountered no one teaching ethics who declared his or her express purpose to be that of indoctrination, a few teachers did report pressures from administrators, colleagues, and professional societies to move in precisely that direction. At a few denominational and other types of institutions, teachers reported that they were expected to advance the specific values of those institutions. In other types of institutions, complaints were directed at those teaching ethics on the grounds that their courses were too analytical, too theoretical, or too detached, and thus failed to advance the particular moral or political causes in which their colleagues passionately believed. Those were scattered reports only, and we were unable to determine to what extent classes on ethics are occasions for indoctrination. Our strong impression, however, is that this is quite rare. Despite a pervasive worry about the problem, very few actual examples were offered to us.

A major difficulty in grappling with the problem of "indoctrination'' is that of gaining a clear sense of what people mean when they use the term. Is it simply the manifestation of bias in the classroom, or is it a penalizing of students for a failure to agree with the professor, or is it a manifest or latent assumption on the part of the professor—duly conveyed to students—that there is one and only one possible true set of answers to ethical problems? We think it most helpful to define "indoctrination" in the following way: a systematic attempt to persuade students of the validity of a belief system, one that (a) radically rules out the possibility of accepting other belief systems; (b) in a deliberate fashion, involves withholding from students either serious objections to that system or those tools of analysis that would enable the student to see its flaws; (c) excludes the possibility of rejection of the belief system; and (d) penalizes deviation. Indoctrination can be said to be the aim of a professor who explicitly attempts to have students accept a closed belief system, one that is not self-critical, and which systematically excludes the possibility of it being rejected. It is all the more dangerous if the professor has the means also of enticing or coercing students into accepting the system.

In that respect, the greatest worry is focused on either religious or political indoctrination. Many hold that by nature religious systems or comparable secular ideological systems rest on premises to be accepted as a matter of faith, and that they are systematically hostile to outside criticism or attempts to force them to justify their premises rationally. Moreover, there seems to be a constant confusion between religion and ethics, as if ethics of necessity reduces to religious beliefs or depends upon them for its foundations.

While it is certainly the case that the moral beliefs of many persons in our society do rest upon religious beliefs, and that all great religions have developed moral principles and codes of conduct, it is by no means the case that this is the only basis for ethical thinking. On the contrary, an equally strong tradition of philosophical and political thought on morality draws its inspiration from very different sources and represents an attempt to develop ethical theory and moral rules independently of religious beliefs. Historically, to be sure, these two traditions have constantly intermixed, and each has drawn from the other to a considerable degree. But they are distinct traditions, and ethics can be and is taught from a philosophical, as distinct from a religious, point of view.

With the possible (and only that) exception of denominational schools, where it is often made perfectly explicit upon entrance that a particular system of morality will be espoused and taught, we believe any teaching of ethics that undertakes to indoctrinate students in the sense noted above is totally unacceptable. This is by no means to cast doubt on the validity of courses in religious ethics. As long as the premises of those courses are made clear, and as long as those courses admit of the tension between different religious beliefs—and the tension as well with nonreligious beliefs—they pose no special problem.

The definition of "indoctrination" provided above might be characterized as one of "hard" indoctrination. But can indoctrination not come in softer, less obvious forms? Three types of soft indoctrination might be noted. The most subtle would be that of methodological indoctrination, that is, pressing upon students one methodology at the expense of all others, and a methodology whose net result is to lead in the direction of one kind of ethical outcome rather than another. We believe it important that professors be sensitive to this problem, that they expose students to methodologies other than those they personally hold, and that students be made aware of the difference variant methodologies can make in the results of moral reasoning.

Another form of soft indoctrination might be characterized as one whereby the professor promotes the view that some moral issues are so much more important than others that the rest can simply be ignored, or that certain evils and outrages are so characteristic of the society that they, and only they, merit the attention of the morally concerned. No doubt some issues *are* comparatively more important than others, and no doubt injustice, racism, sexism, and exploitation—to mention a list of common evils—are abroad in the society. Nonetheless, for a professor to systematically press his or her own version of the greatest evils, or what *the* real issues are, is as much a disservice to students as pressing upon them a particular methodology. Students should have the opportunity of being exposed to different notions of what constitute the most important moral issues, and in particular, exposed to those other versions that fly in the face of the professor's own convictions.

Finally, we would note what could easily be the most obvious possibility of soft indoctrination, assuming professors are already prepared to reject the other forms. That would simply be the design of syllabi that would express a bias or predilection on the part of the professor. There can be no such thing as a "value-free" course in ethics any more than in other subjects. Nonetheless, professors have a duty to seek impartiality. The best way this can be done is by making certain that reading lists contain a diversity of subject matter and viewpoints, a diversity sufficient to enable students to have immediately at hand material that will enable them to pit one view against the other.

We believe that a course in ethics at the undergraduate or the professional school level should send students forth to think about ethical issues on their own. That task cannot be accomplished unless the teacher supplies the students with those tools of ethical analysis that will enable them to critique, and to be in a position to reject, not only their present moral convictions, but also those of the teacher. Teachers should feel perfectly free to express their own moral convictions. At the very least, this can be helpful to students—to see how someone, who has presumably thought more systematically and over a long period about morality, frames arguments and justifies his or her own position. But it is no less important that the teacher supply the student with those analytic tools and a range of reading matter that will enable the student to develop an independent stance. With respect to indoctrination, the test of the teaching of ethics is not whether students end by sharing the convictions of their teachers, but whether they have come to those convictions by means of the use of skills that might have led in other directions and may do so in the future.

Indoctrination is a danger in any course, for other courses as well will shape student attitudes, beliefs, and behavior. One may grant that undergraduates are often less mature than professional students, and perhaps more malleable. For all that, the very idea and purpose of higher education is to enable students to establish their own moral and intellectual outlook. That undergraduates may be somewhat more prone to be influenced by their teachers is probably inevitable. For just that reason, then, professors in all courses have a special obligation to move their students toward the goal of independence; and that would certainly be true in courses in ethics, which might under some circumstances have a more decisive role in shaping fundamental values than would other courses.

As much as we believe in the value of teaching ethics, however, more than a touch of reality is necessary in assessing any worries that these courses might be too influential, and make altogether too much difference, in the lives of the students. A simple fact of life is that no single course or even a series of courses in ethics will be the sole moral influence on students. They will bring with them the values of their families, experience a variety of values and moral conflicts through the media and other sources, be influenced by their professors in other courses, and constantly be challenged by their fellow students. There will be, in short, many antidotes to a course in ethics (if one cares to look upon it that way), and many other possibilities to analyze critically what they receive in their ethics course.

C. Qualifications for the Teaching of Ethics

The recent rise of interest in the teaching of ethics has drawn teachers from every imaginable discipline. Perhaps the most distinctive feature of the broad field, one which sharply differentiates it from almost every other area in higher education, is that many of those now teaching the subject were not originally trained to do so.

The principal reason for considering the qualifications of those who teach ethics is a concern for the quality of that teaching. Courses in ethics should be taught with the same rigor and background store of knowledge as any other course; hence, qualifications are critical. Recently renewed interest in ethics at the undergraduate and professional school level has drawn heavily on those trained in ethics. But it has also attracted some with no special professional qualifications at all. This is particularly true in many of the courses taught at the professional school level, and in many undergraduate courses on science and ethics, bioethics, and journalism.

Whatever the shortcomings of a training in philosophical or theological ethics, it normally provides some well-established criteria for assessing and justifying moral arguments and some body of developed theory to provide a grounding for applied ethics. There are, in short, disciplinary standards of rigor and quality. A total absence of some disciplinary standards can be disastrous. Enthusiasm, good will, and interest are not sufficient qualifications for teaching courses in organic chemistry, micro-economics, or Greek literature. There is no reason why they should be thought sufficient for the teaching of ethics, a difficult subject with a long history.

It is no less important to point out that good training in the technical aspects of biology, law, or public policy, even supplemented by considerable practical experience, does not automatically confer any special skill in analyzing or resolving the moral dilemmas arising in those fields. It is seductive to think they do. Most thoughtful practitioners will have wrestled with moral problems, will have discussed them with colleagues, and may well in their undergraduate education, or in their own efforts in self-education, have given some thought to ethical theory and analysis. That, however, is not sufficient for teaching a course in ethics—any more than the personal experience of having balanced a checkbook and the daily perusal of the financial section of the newpaper qualifies one to teach a course in economics.

What ought to count as adequate qualifications?[58] We want to reject that form of disciplinary chauvinism which contends that only those with advanced degrees in moral philosophy or moral theology are properly prepared. They are surely the only ones properly qualified to teach courses that fall strictly and entirely within their own disciplines. But the matter is very different for the teaching of applied ethics and professional ethics. It is at this point that the field becomes, of necessity, interdisciplinary, requiring knowledge both of ethics and of the other field or fields to be analyzed from an ethical perspective. It is ethics *and* law, ethics *and* biology, ethics *and* journalism. A person trained exclusively in ethics will not be fully qualified to teach those courses; other knowledge will have to be acquired. Yet, by the same token, someone trained in the discipline other than ethics can become qualified to teach applied or professional ethics if, in addition to training in his or her own field, additional grounding is acquired in ethics. A philosopher without any exposure to the field of journalism is not qualified to teach ethics and journalism—and an expert in journalism does not qualify to teach the subject without some exposure to philosophical ethics. A traditional distinction should make the point clear: when the teaching of ethics requires the knowledge of two or more fields, it is a necessary but not sufficient condition that there be a full grounding in one of the fields; a sufficient condition would be some degree of grounding in the other field as well.

How much and what kind of education is necessary to achieve that kind of "sufficient condition" for the teaching of applied or professional ethics? Ideally, perhaps, someone who teaches such a course should have both a Ph.D in philosophical or theological ethics and a degree in another, pertinent field. But that is not often a practical solution, nor is it usually necessary. Other ways of becoming adequately grounded in a field in addition to one's own may be perfectly sufficient.

What do we mean by "adequately grounded?" Such grounding would require a broad familiarity with the language, concepts, and characteristic modes of analysis of another discipline—what that discipline considers to be an appropriate way of handling issues that arise in its field, how it makes use of evidence or data and evaluates them, how it distinguishes between good work and bad, between the brilliant and the average. How much training is necessary for this purpose? We propose that at least one year of education should be aimed for, whether gained in one bloc or cumulatively. Some are undoubtedly able to educate themselves entirely; but most need to work, at least for a time, with those trained in the other field.

No less important, those so trained should have a decent sense of the internal dynamics of the other discipline. It is evident, for example, that all disciplines and professions display a gap between the idealized or theoretical version of their work and what actually occurs in practice. Writings on the philosophy of science are not necessarily good guides to what researchers actually do in laboratories. Textbooks on differential diagnosis rarely reveal the mixture of art, intuition, and experience that mark the first-rate diagnostician. Just as practicing lawyers take pleasure in pointing out to new law clerks the difference between the "real world" of law and what they learned in school, so too almost all practitioners in every field make analogous points. Thus, some degree of personal exposure—in the clinic, in the courtroom, in the newspaper office or television studio—is almost always necessary. Not only is it imperative to have some familiarity with the theories of other fields, but it is equally important to have a familiarity with the practical moral problems as they arise in the work or professional context.

We want to deny the necessity of a full graduate training in ethics as a condition for teaching courses in applied and professional ethics. Yet we also want to contend that the field of ethics should have a privileged place in the background and preparation of any teacher of such a course. By a "privileged place" we mean simply that no one can claim competence to teach ethics without some familiarity with the history, the modes of reasoning, and the concepts of moral philosophy or moral theology. That would seem such an obvious point that one might wonder whether it needs making at all. Unfortunately, whether because of a resistance to grappling with moral theory, or because a number of fields include within their domain the study of "values" (particularly in education and the social sciences), many teachers appear to feel no strong compulsion to familiarize themselves with moral philosophy or moral theology. We believe this to be a serious mistake. Those who have not made a strong effort to become familiar with the field of ethics cannot be expected to teach rigorous and well-grounded courses, whether theoretical, applied, or professional.

A common solution to the problem of qualifications is that of team-teaching. Its attractions are obvious. It provides those teachers lacking specialized training in another discipline an opportunity to rely upon a colleague to provide students that knowledge they do not have. It can also provide for students a vivid sense of what it means to try combining two or more disciplines in pursuit of a common problem and mutual insights. There are also some drawbacks. It is an expensive solution, often an impractical one because of the departmental structure of most colleges and universities, and it is obviously dependent upon finding professors who can work well together. Perhaps its main drawback, however, is that it is all too easy simply to present material from different disciplines in a parallel, side-by-side way, with little effort to achieve a full integration.

Two conditions seem imperative for good team-teaching. The first is that the courses be structured in a way that weaves together as tightly as possible the technical material from the non-ethics discipline with the material that is squarely in the field of ethics. The second is that those engaged in team-teaching be fully prepared themselves to grapple with material from their colleague's discipline. The initial goal of team-teaching efforts should be that of the mutual education of the instructors. If they cannot find ways of educating each other, it is hardly likely that their students will make the necessary connections. Team-teaching should not become a substitute for the more important task of a teacher's developing a decent grounding in another field. Team-teaching can enhance that possibility, but given the practical and other difficulties of organizing and sustaining on a permanent basis interdisciplinary courses, most teachers of ethics will eventually be forced to go it alone.

The most serious lack at present is that of training programs for those who teach ethics in all the kinds of courses we have discussed. There are at present few carefully thought-out training opportunities. Many instructors are inadequately trained, as we have mentioned; yet even they and others have used a great deal of ingenuity in putting together courses and practical experience in order to prepare themselves to teach. The lack grows more serious each year, as the courses in ethics multiply. Without well-organized and sustained formal training programs, we foresee increasing difficulties of credibility and solidity in the teaching of ethics.

D. Evaluation of the Teaching of Ethics

The subject of evaluation is a frustrating and irritating one.[59] This is partly because many of the hard questions about ethical instruction—what counts as ethics, what are the legitimate goals of ethics teaching, how can indoctrination be avoided—are often left for those in charge of doing evaluations to answer. Also, the irritation and frustration spring partly from the feeling that courses on ethics and values are unfairly singled out for evaluative scrutiny. Few other courses in the curriculum receive the critical attention that new courses on ethics and values do.

If we take as a tentative list of goals the ability to recognize and identify ethical and value issues in various contexts, the development of analytical skills, the mastery of a certain amount of ethical and value theory, and the ability to apply such theory to specific problems or matters of moral and value dispute, then it becomes possible to ask the question: How should the success of courses which try to attain these goals be measured?

Most individuals teaching in the humanities feel that they do, in fact, have standards of evaluation that allow them to note and reward competence and excellence in humanistic work. Normally, there is a good deal of evaluative feedback between students and teachers in courses on ethics and values offered in traditional departments of philosophy and theology. Classroom discussions, tests, writing assignments of various sorts, and student-teacher conferences, all provide students with ample opportunities to have their nascent analytical ethical skills and value beliefs critically assessed and discussed by faculty members. Classroom performance, quizzes or tests, the compilation of diaries or workbooks, and written papers and essays are the traditional modes for applying the criteria of competence and excellence for evaluation in courses in the humanities in general, and in particular, in courses on ethics and values. The real issue concerning evaluation, then, is not so much whether modes of evaluation exist for humanities courses, but whether the traditional means of doing evaluations in the humanities will suffice for instruction that emphasizes ethics in applied and professional school contexts.

We see little reason for thinking that the traditional modes of evaluation will not suffice when it comes to teaching ethics and values in new or applied contexts. The easiest way of telling whether a student has acquired analytical skills in argumentation or has mastered a body of ethical knowledge to the point where it can easily be applied to the solution of cases is to observe the student in classroom discussion and to read examples of the student's written work. The ability to identify ethical issues, to apply theory to practice, and to show a mastery of ethical theory can all be ascertained by instructors who carefully attend to what students say in class and on paper. Admittedly, such evaluation modes require close faculty supervision of students and a good deal of homework for both faculty and students. In some circumstances it may be appropriate and helpful to arrange for evaluations by outside examiners, who would be experienced teachers, but who may not have taught the students being evaluated. The most important point, however, is that traditional evaluation modalities are available for those who choose to use them in attempting to teach in the area of ethics.

Still, it might be objected that it is not clear what counts as good or competent work in ethics. The fact is that the standards of logic and argumentation are no different in ethics than they are in any other part of inquiry. Good arguments are good arguments whether they are phrased or couched in the language of values or couched in the language of facts. Objectivity is not jeopardized simply by the nature of the subject matter of ethics and values instruction. Students can be taught what counts as an acceptable and an unacceptable argument in ethics. Ad hominem arguments, logically fallacious arguments, tu quoque arguments, arguments from authority are all to be rejected as acceptable means of ethical argumentation. Logical coherence and factual adequacy are the linchpins of acceptable performance in ethics. If this is so, then there would seem to be little problem with making clear the standards of evaluation that ought to be used in assessing the attainment of espoused goals in ethical and value instruction.

E. Teaching Techniques and Course Organization

1. The Pedagogy of the Teaching of Ethics

Like most others who teach, those who teach ethics often wish there was a certain and simple way to instruct students effectively. But teaching is an art: there are no guaranteed ways to teach courses on ethics, any more than other courses, successfully. Teachers have different personal skills and inclinations, and they must often teach a wide range of students, who vary in their capacity, background, and interests. Since the teaching of ethics takes place at both the undergraduate and professional school level, the pedagogical skills and approaches that might be pertinent at one level might be much less so at another. An undergraduate course in bioethics will require special efforts to evoke a feel for dilemmas in biomedicine that may be less necessary in a medical school, where students will see the issues directly; and what may be effective with medical students may not be equally so with law students. Inevitably, teachers must find their own way, and it may often be necessary to change their approach from one class to another, or from one teaching context to another. At the least, those teaching ethics should convey both enthusiasm and seriousness and, in particular, a willingness to lead students patiently through what can be difficult material, complicated moral dilemmas, and a passion-charged subject matter.

The most common problem facing the teacher of ethics is that of achieving a suitable balance between theoretical material and case studies. Applied and professional ethics focus attention on working through very difficult, concrete ethical problems and dilemmas. The use of case studies, and of concrete examples, is obviously necessary and helpful in that process. Cases may be approached in an ad hoc fashion, to illustrate this or that general point, or they may be approached in a more systematic way—by grouping cases under general thematic topics. For instance, the subject of distributive justice might be approached by drawing upon case examples from the allocation of scarce medical resources, by examples from urban policies, or by court cases involving reverse discrimination. On the whole, case studies are employed most effectively when they can readily be used to draw out broader ethical principles and moral rules. In many fields, the use of historical cases can be particularly helpful; they are real, not invented, and can be followed from beginning to end.

The greatest hazards in the use of case examples are those of getting distracted by non-ethical issues, by a fastening upon case studies exclusively for their own sake, and by allowing the sheer drama of many cases to overcome the more serious need for sober analysis. A skillful teacher of ethics should try to avoid those pitfalls and make use of cases in order to draw the attention of students to the common elements in a variety of cases, and to the implicit problems of ethical theory to which they may point. Questions of duty and obligation arise in many contexts; for example, the obligations of doctors toward patients and lawyers toward clients share a number of common features (and show some differences as well). Although it is of course important that individual cases be taken seriously—for that is the way most moral dilemmas arise—it is no less important to assist students to develop the skills necessary to generalize from cases, to recognize new ethical dilemmas when they encounter them, and to have developed teaching strategies that allow cases to be approached in an orderly way.

One shortcoming of the case method is that students invariably seek more facts, in the belief that if only one knew more about the case, one could easily resolve the ethical dilemma. Alternatively, students often try to make the ethical dilemma go away by "patching up" the case suitably. Part of the teacher's task should be to indicate that more facts need not make the case easier to resolve; they may make it even more complex, therefore harder. It is also useful for teachers to insist that the facts of the case be left as stated, thereby forcing students to come to grips with the hard problems they will eventually face as practicing professionals (or as moral agents).

Another common problem with using cases in a classroom setting is that students tend to pass the buck when it comes time to offer a solution to a troubling moral problem. Since it is, after all, a classroom, it is easy for students to avoid the difficult task of attempting a resolution. One useful technique is to break a class into small groups of, say, five to eight students. Cases can be constructed in such a manner that there is a moral decision to be made, and the small groups then go off by themselves and grapple with the problem. Later, each group presents its decision in the case, along with the reasons for its choice. This technique not only allows for a systematic exchange of ideas among students; it also points up that even after ample time for discussion and reflection, reasonable people may disagree about what is the right thing to do.

Most teachers of applied and professional ethics believe that the best way to begin a course of ethics is by examining cases. Many philosophers, in particular, report that they learned this the hard way, for their initial inclination was to begin with broad ethical principles and only later introduce cases. Few reported the latter to be an effective way of teaching, especially in applied and professional ethics. However, one can only generalize here, and we encountered during our study a number of teachers who reported a very successful introduction to applied and professional ethics by means of an exploration of ethical theories and concepts. Many teachers also reported a successful use of role-playing, of formal classroom debates, and of film and television presentations. What works effectively for some teachers does not seem helpful to others. Like case studies, media presentations can serve to evoke emotions and make much more concrete cases that would be far less dramatic if they appeared on the printed page. Yet some teachers reported that they came eventually to use fewer audio-visual presentations, primarily because they found that their dramatic impact served more to arouse passion than to facilitate solid analysis.

Whatever the teaching technique used, it is critically important that students receive an introduction to the serious literature on ethics. They should come to know that there is such a literature, that others have wrestled seriously with the problems they are encountering for the first time, and that a familiarity with the literature is most likely to serve them best in the long run. We encountered many courses which seemed to depend excessively upon the use of newspaper articles, or articles from popular magazines. Often they were chosen simply because they were short, pithy, and raised very directly specific ethical issues. But too often that kind of reading matter was not supported by more serious books and articles.

The best source of potential information on the pedagogical problems of the teaching of ethics is the experience of other teachers. Notes and ideas should be exchanged, the strategies used by others might be experimented with, and on-site observations of the way in which colleagues conduct classes can also be helpful. (Unfortunately, in many schools, those teaching ethics have few if any colleagues; they are usually forced to turn to meetings of professional associations to find others to talk with.) Too often those who receive graduate degrees, and who plan to teach, receive very little direct instruction in the art of teaching as part of their graduate studies. This is as true in the field of ethics, theoretical or applied, as it is in every other field. What is needed is intensive interaction and discussion among those who actually teach.

For all the importance of an imaginative and sensible means of course organization and teaching techniques, the personal deportment of the teacher may be of far greater importance. We can do no better here than to quote these words of Martin Trow: "What is common to those teachers who have an impact on the moral life of their students by serving as models of the intellectual virtues is that as teachers they resist successfully the powerful pulls of routine. Very much, perhaps most, teaching at any level is a fairly routine organization of information and skills packaged for delivery to students who do not yet have them. Only occasionally do most of us 'come alive' in the classroom and present to our students not merely what our disciplines purport to know but how they actually work, and demonstrate with what qualities of spirit and feeling these hard-won insights and understandings have been gained. But teachers who serve as powerful models differ from the rest of us in the consistency with which they exhibit these qualities, the consistency with which they are genuinely alive in the classroom, actually experiencing, as if for the first time, the joys of discovery or the rigors of analysis. . . . What is so impressive to those fortunate enough to study with these teachers is precisely this consistency of live response to familiar material; it seems to demonstrate that their teaching reflects not what they are paid to do, but what they are, and that way it expands our conception of the possibilities of human life.''[60]

2. Where Should Ethics Be Taught in the Curriculum?

The question of the appropriate placement of courses and programs in ethics in the curriculum is a troubling one. It is often a concrete and practical problem, since in many institutions it will be possible to have only one course on ethics, with no assurance that students will have a chance thereafter to grapple directly and systematically with moral problems. For others, even if there are not severe constraints of time and money, there is still the question of the most appropriate place to introduce ethics. Moreover, an answer that might be suitable at the professional school level might be irrelevant or wrong in undergraduate colleges.

We can propose no single, general answer to that question of the "best" placement of ethics courses; practical considerations will often prove decisive in many, if not most, institutions. It is, however, possible to speak in terms of ideals, and in this context some general suggestions can be offered. The most important point is that all students, in both the undergraduate and professional schools, should have the opportunity for a *systematic* exposure to ethics, an exposure equivalent to at least one semester's duration. We emphasize the word "systematic" in order to underscore our belief that students should have a sustained chance to understand the nature of ethics, and to grasp the relationship between ethical theory and practical moral dilemmas. Put another way, they should have the opportunity to develop a coherent view of the nature of ethics, and be afforded a glimpse into its whole domain. Only a well-organized course in ethics is likely to achieve that goal. Yet it helps if students encounter explicit discussions of moral dilemmas in other courses as well. Advanced courses should also be available for those who wish to pursue the subject in greater depth. Although all students should have access to a systematic exposure to ethics, some will want to pursue it more fully, and some (particularly in professional schools) may want to make it a continuing part of their professional career. If possible, these students should have the opportunity to do advanced work, even in a professional school context. This may be important, not only for their intellectual development, but because such advanced courses can serve to develop certain individuals who will take positions of leadership in their professional fields in the future.

One medical school provided a week-long introduction to ethics during the first year, segments of other courses devoted to ethics during both the first and second year, and an advanced and intensive elective seminar for fourth-year students. The principle of that program was that students should have a repeated exposure to ethics, with further work a possibility for the most interested. With adaptations, that is a solid possible model for many professional schools. Given a choice, it is perhaps a more effective model that that of a school that simply offers one course, but provides no other occasions for a vigorous discussion of ethical issues.

A common problem in professional schools is whether it is better, comparatively, to introduce ethics at the beginning of a professional education, or to wait until the end. The main argument for introducing it at the beginning is to alert students to the ethical problems they will encounter in other courses, and to serve notice of the importance of ethical concerns. The argument for putting it at the end of a professional education is that, by then, students will better understand the nature of their profession and its problems, and thus be in a stronger position to appreciate the moral dilemmas—something not always possible when students, at the very beginning, have yet to really discover the nature of the professional problems themselves. Opinion is divided on this point, and both approaches have worked well at different schools.

A frequent comment, at both the undergraduate and especially the professional school level, is that ethics ought not to be taught in a specific course at all, but should be built into all other courses in the curriculum. The participants in our project came to call this the "pervasive method." Its attractions are understandable. It takes account of the fact that ethical problems arise in almost all areas and domains of human activity, and that in the university they should be dealt with, at least to some extent, in all courses. It also recognizes an unfortunate tendency in higher education, that of isolating an important topic in a single course and then otherwise ignoring the subject in the rest of the curriculum.

Despite the apparent power of some of those contentions, we were persuaded by our survey of the present teaching of ethics, and by the experience of a large number of schools, to reject the "pervasive method" if it is the sole method of grappling with ethical problems. First, no other serious subject is taught in that fashion; that is, considered so important that it is taught in all courses in general, but in none in particular. Why should ethics be made an exception to a general rule in higher education—that if a subject is important, then it should have a course in its own right? Second, many of those who espouse the introduction of ethics in every course are prepared to concede that it simply does not happen in most courses. There is no reason to expect that all professors who are asked to take up ethical problems in their courses will actually do so—we have been able to discover no institutions in which it has happened. Third, even if professors were persuaded that they should give over part of their course to ethical problems, there is no reason to believe that most would have any special competence to do so.

The training of most professionals gives them no systematic background in ethics, much less enough of a background to allow them to handle ethical issues as competently as they handle issues in their own professional fields. There is no reason to expect that most professors would care to give a significant segment of their courses to the ethical problems of their disciplines. Most have heavy enough responsibilities as it is. With the "pervasive method," students do not bring up many issues, and faculty devote little time to discussing those that do come up. Perhaps most important, the diffusion of ad hoc ethical analysis among a wide variety of courses deprives students of the opportunity to focus systematically on ethical problems for their own sake, and also of a context for giving them a coherent means of developing broader views on the nature of ethics.

For all of these reasons, we think students should have at least one well-organized, reasonably long course in ethics at both the undergraduate and the professional school level. Otherwise, they will not be able to grasp the seriousness and complexity of the subject or acquire the tools for dealing with ethical problems. This is not to deny that it would be highly useful for ethical problems to be introduced in other courses, or to be made regular segments of some courses. It is only to say that some well-developed courses are needed in order that the students will be in a good position to understand, and to analyze adequately, the ethical problems they will encounter in other aspects of their education. If there are such courses, students will bring up in other courses ethical issues they perceive; and faculty members will have someone to turn to with questions and concerns. The entire institution will benefit if someone is actively teaching and writing on ethical issues.

3. The University as a Context for the Teaching of Ethics

Universities shape and influence in a variety of ways the

teaching of ethics that goes on within them. The university is an institutional setting which determines whether, where, and how ethics will be taught. Its rules and organizational patterns determine, for example, whether courses on ethics are confined to departments of philosophy or religion or are offered in other academic departments or in interdisciplinary courses. The outcome of that process will vary in universities that appear to have very similar values and goals, and will be shaped by their different patterns of academic organization and internal politics. An understanding of those forces is not irrelevant to the future, in particular, of applied ethics and professional ethics.

The possibility of introducing new courses on ethics into the university is thus influenced both by its values and the ways in which it makes decisions. The tradition (or, as some would have it, the myth) of "value-free" science and scholarship can be highly significant. So far as scholars and scientists believe that their subjects are governed by their own internal laws and values, they may see the teaching of ethics in those departments as a way of smuggling "external values" and purposes into the autonomous life of their disciplines. This is not the same as a fear of indoctrination; rather, it might be thought of as a fear of "contamination" or "distraction"—students who should be learning mathematics or physics or history are side-tracked into archaic and useless discussions of ethical issues. Many scientists and scholars see the progress of their own discipline as marked by its liberation from structures of belief, religious or philosophical, extrinsic to their fields. And they may feel that courses on ethics merely reintroduce long-dead and irrelevant questions into their subjects. These scholars may suspect that many students are truly interested in the moral and ethical questions of their disciplines; but they may also feel, not wholly without reason, that many of these same students would prefer to chat about the values and assumptions of the disciplines rather than actually learn those disciplines.

Those concerns are muted when ethics courses are taught in and confined to departments of philosophy and religion where, as most academics acknowledge, they are an "appropriate" part of the subject. But outside the departments of philosophy and religion, the suspicion that a course on ethics is part of the broad trend toward the softening or evasion of academic standards is widespread among college and university teachers. These concerns will continue to affect the departments that offer such courses, the kinds of courses that are offered, even when they are permitted, and the kinds of academic persons who come forward to teach them. Even when departments accede to student demands and other pressures for the introduction of courses on ethics into their curriculum, they may, in fact, express their disapproval by putting those courses into a kind of disciplinary ghetto. That is often as effective a sanction against the introduction of new subjects into a discipline as an outright refusal to teach those subjects. If ethics courses are to avoid this fate, it is helpful, where possible, that they be introduced into the university by respected senior professors, those who have made their academic reputation in the mainstream of their own disciplines. The auspices under which such courses are introduced into the university are often decisive for their future survival and incorporation into the curriculum.

Universities are not only a political context for decisions about the introduction of courses on applied ethics. They are also the moral context for research scholarship and teaching, a place where, in fact, values are continually being created, transmitted, shaped, modified, rewarded, or violated. But these values and the institutions that embody and serve them exist alongside many other activities and purposes, some of which are competitive with scholarship and teaching for resources, some of which are in principle divergent from them. Many moral issues arise in the life of the university and of its members. These issues, personally and often painfully experienced by students, can be a part of the content of courses in applied ethics. Unlike moral dilemmas experienced vicariously and through writings, the problems experienced by undergraduates and professional students in their own academic lives will reveal the complexity, the flavor, the contingent quality, that marks all real moral dilemmas, but which so often escapes from the discussion of moral predicaments reported at second- or third-hand.

IV. Summary Recommendations

American higher education is in the throes of many difficulties at present. These include declining enrollments, increasing financial pressure, the inability of many promising teachers and scholars to gain employment or tenure, and some degree of public criticism. It may not be an auspicious moment to urge the introduction of new courses and programs, whether in ethics or any other subject. Nonetheless, we do not hesitate to propose that the teaching of ethics be given a far more central role in the curriculum than it has had in recent decades. While many of the current problems of higher education are practical and financial, others bear on the nature and role of the university itself. Few persons would openly contend that the main purpose of higher education, even of an explicitly professional education, is simply that of preparing students for better jobs and higher incomes. Yet, for many students, that is the perceived reality. Nor would many educators or others contend that questions of ethics and values should have no place in the university. Most would assert, in a very general way, just the opposite. Yet the formal opportunities to pursue moral questions are often scant and episodic. Few would argue that the professions do not have moral purposes and traditions, or deny that professionals ought to serve goals that transcend the merely technical. Yet the opportunities to examine the nature of the professions and their moral purposes are scant.

Those discrepancies were a stimulus for our project. Much more important, the same discrepancies underlie a general public uneasiness about the directions of higher education, and a no less strong uneasiness within the academic community itself. One need look no further than the variety of curriculum reform movements and faculty renewal programs now underway to lend credence to that assertion. We have centered our attention on one aspect only of the current ferment: that of the role of ethics instruction in the university. But it is an aspect that reflects a more general concern about the university and the way it is preparing students to manage their own lives, their life in community with others, and their vocational or professional roles. More and better courses in ethics will by no means solve the larger problems facing the university, nor will a focus on moral issues guarantee it a new purpose and vitality. Our only claim is that a "higher education" that does not foster, support, and implement an examination of the moral life will fail its own purposes, the needs of its students, and the welfare of society. The university offers a unique context for a careful examination of moral claims and moral purposes. We ask only that such an examination be made formal and explicit, and that sufficient imagination, energy, and resources be invested in the teaching of ethics that its importance will become manifest, both within and outside the university.

We have already set forth the substance of our findings, our recommendations, and our suggestions; we hope that those who desire a fuller discussion will turn to the other publications prepared as part of our project. Still, it may serve an additional purpose if we summarize those recommendations we believe to be the most important.

1. *Goals in the Teaching of Ethics.* The general purpose of the teaching of ethics ought to be that of stimulating the moral imagination, developing skills in the recognition and analysis of moral issues, eliciting a sense of moral obligation and personal responsibility, and learning both to tolerate—and to resist—moral disagreement and ambiguity. Those purposes ought to mark all courses in ethics; they should be supplemented by the examination of those specific topics appropriate to particular areas of personal, social, and professional concern.

Courses in ethics ought not explicitly to seek behavioral change in students. They should seek to assist students in the development of those insights, skills, and perspectives that set the stage for a life of personal moral responsibility, manifesting careful and serious moral reflection.

The undergraduate teaching of ethics ought to assist students in the formation of their personal values and moral ideals, to introduce them to the broad range of moral problems facing their society and the world, to provide them contact with important ethical theories and moral traditions, and to give them the opportunity to wrestle with problems of applied ethics, whether personal or professional.

The teaching of ethics in professional schools ought to prepare future professionals to understand the kinds of moral issues they are likely to confront in their chosen vocations, to introduce them to the moral ideals of their profession, and to assist them in understanding the relationship between their professional work and that of the broader values and needs of the society.

2. *Pluralism and Indoctrination.* Courses in ethics should respect the pluralistic principles of our society, acknowledging the variety of moral perspectives that mark different religious and other groups. Indoctrination, whether political, theological, ideological, or philosophical, is wholly out of place in the teaching of ethics. Although students should be assisted in developing moral ideals and fashioning a coherent way of approaching ethical theory and moral dilemmas, the task of the teacher is not to promote a special set of values, but only to promote those sensitivities and analytical skills necessary to help students reach their own moral judgments.

3. *Evaluation of the Teaching of Ethics.* The most appropriate methods of evaluation are those traditional to the humanities: an assessment on the part of teachers (and in some cases outside examiners) about whether their students understand key concepts, are able to fashion coherent moral arguments, both orally and in writing, and can display an ability to recognize moral problems sensitively and examine them in a rational way. While empirical and other test instruments can have value in measuring changes in student judgment of moral issues, it is doubtful that they can be as useful or illuminating as the ordinary means of evaluating the progress made by students in ethics courses.

4. *Qualifications for the Teaching of Ethics.* An advanced de-

gree in philosophy or religion is the minimal standard for ethics courses taught within the disciplinary perspectives of those fields. As an ideal, those teaching applied and professional ethics— where knowledge of one or more fields is necessary—ought to have the equivalent of one year of training in the field in which they were not initially trained. Team-teaching, in addition to its other values, can often help fill the gap when one or more of the instructors has been trained in one field only. Courses in applied and professional ethics ought not to be introduced into the curriculum unless those proposing to teach such courses have the necessary training or are in the process of getting it. As a general rule, the more deeply a teacher proposes to go into the subject matter of applied and professional ethics, the greater the degree of training that will be necessary. By the same token, extensive training will not ordinarily be necessary for those who propose only to give over a short segment of a course to one or more issues in applied or professional ethics.

5. *Training Programs in Applied and Professional Ethics.* The most important general need in the field of applied and professional ethics is the development of training programs. At present, there are very few opportunities for those trained in one field to gain the equivalent of the one year of additional training proposed above. Training programs of two kinds are needed: first, programs to assist those with no training in ethics to gain a basic knowledge of that field, and second, programs for those trained in ethics that would allow them to work for the equivalent of a year in another field. While a few joint Ph.D. programs, providing degrees in two fields, would be helpful, the more critical need is for one-year programs, or for a series of summer programs or workshops that would, over a period of time, provide the equivalent of one year of training. Our research and questionnaires for this project indicate there would be a significant audience for such programs.

6. *The Placing of Ethics in the Curriculum.* Every undergraduate should have a systematic exposure to both ethical theory and applied ethics. The minimal standard ought to be that of a one-semester course, with other opportunities available for more advanced work in ethical theory or work in different areas of applied or professional ethics. Every professional student should

have a systematic exposure to the ethical problems of his or her chosen profession.

While moral problems ought to be faced when they arise in the context of other courses at the undergraduate or professional school level, reliance should not be placed upon such sporadic encounters as a substitute for the availability of well-organized, full courses. No other serious subject is taught in the curriculum by what has been called the "pervasive method," and ethics ought not to be the outcast.

7. *Establishing a Climate for Courses in Ethics.* Those proposing to teach courses in ethics should fully inform their colleagues and pertinent administrators of the purposes and expectations of their courses. It should not be assumed that others will automatically understand the explicit purpose of such courses. Special efforts should be made to explain to the university or professional school community what courses in ethics hope to achieve, and the means to be used to achieve them.

Notes

1. "Traditional Values Favored," *The Gallup Poll* (Princeton, N.J.: American Institute of Public Opinion, June 22, 1978).

2. Carnegie Council on Policy Studies in Higher Education, *Fair Practices in Higher Education: Rights and Responsibilities of Students in their Colleges in a Period of Intensified Competition for Enrollment* (San Francisco: Jossey-Bass, 1979).

3. Quoted in Edward B. Fiske, "Ethics Courses Now Attracting More U.S. College Students," *New York Times,* February 20, 1978.

4. Michael Walzer, "Teaching Morality," *The New Republic,* June 10, 1978, p. 13.

5. Derek C. Bok, "Can Ethics Be Taught?" *Change*, October 1976, p. 30.

6. Martin Trow, "Higher Education and Moral Development," *AAUP Bulletin,* Spring 1976, p. 20.

7. Questions of course organization and pedagogical technique are taken up in a number of the other papers and studies of The Teaching of Ethics Project of The Hastings Center, listed in the Bibliography.

8. Richard C. Morrill, "Alternatives in Moral and Values Education," in *Values and the Education of Conscience,* chap. 2 (work in progress).

9. Louis Raths, Merrill Harmin, and Sidney Simon, *Values and Teaching* (Columbus: Charles E. Merrill, 1966); Sidney Simon, Leland Howe, and Howard Kirschenbaum, *Values Clarification* (New York: Hart Publishing Co., 1972); Brian Hall, *Value Clarification as Learning Process,* vol. 1, *A Sourcebook,* vol. 11, *A Guidebook of Learning Strategies* (New York: Paulist Press, 1973).

10. Cf. Michael Donnellan and James Ebben, eds., *Values Pedagogy in Higher Education* (Adrian, Michigan: Siena Heights College, 1978); Earl J. McGrath, "Carriers, Values and General Education," *Liberal Education* 60,

1974; Earl J. McGrath, *Values, Liberal Education and National Destiny* (Indianapolis: Lilly Endowment, n.d.). Needless to say, the topic of "values" has also received considerable attention in philosophy and the social sciences.

11. Lawrence Kohlberg and Rochelle Mayer, "Development as the Aim of Education," *Harvard Educational Review* 42 (1972): 449–96; Lawrence Kohlberg, "Moral Stages and Moralization," in Thomas Lickona, ed., *Moral Development and Behavior* (New York: Holt, Rinehart and Winston, 1976), pp. 34–35; Jean Piaget, *The Moral Judgment of the Child* (New York: The Free Press, 1965 [1932]).

12. Our discussions on the nature and scope of ethics were considerably advanced by papers presented at our meetings on the topic "What Is Normative Ethics?" by Kurt Baier, Frederick A. Olafson, and Gene Outka. See William F. Frankena & John T. Granrose, eds., *Introductory Readings in Ethics* (Englewood Cliffs, N.J.: Prentice-Hall, 1974) and Paul Taylor, ed., *Problems in Moral Philosophy: An Introduction to Ethics* (Belmont, California: Dickenson Publishing Co., 1971). For further readings in this area, see Bibliography.

13. Louis Hodges advanced our analysis of applied ethics and its interdisciplinary nature in a paper given at one of our meetings, "Applied Ethics and Pre-Professionals."

14. For a fuller discussion of these issues see William F. May, "Professional Ethics: Setting, Terrain, and Teacher," in *Ethics Teaching in Higher Education*, eds. Daniel Callahan and Sissela Bok, (New York: Plenum Press, 1980).

15. Two of these "cross-professional" conflicts are taken up in greater detail in Callahan and Bok, ibid.

16. Douglas Sloan, "The Teaching of Ethics in the American Undergraduate Curriculum, 1876–1976," in Callahan and Bok, ibid.

17. Ibid.

18. Ibid.

19. We are especially indebted to Carola Mone for her correlations of the data available to us.

20. Bernard Murchland, "Ethics and the Undergraduate Curriculum," paper presented at a meeting of The Teaching of Ethics Project. We are particularly indebted to Professor Murchland for his assistance in our analysis of the teaching of undergraduate ethics.

21. We are particularly indebted to Patricia A. Sullivan for an informative paper she presented at a meeting of The Teaching of Ethics Project, "Science and Ethics: A Focus on Bioethics Teaching." See also Thomas K. McElhinney, ed., *Human Values Teaching Programs for Health Professionals* (Philadelphia: The Society for Health & Human Values, 1976).

22. Joseph M. Dasbach, *EVIST Resource Directory* (Washington, D.C.: American Association for the Advancement of Science, 1978) and Ezra D.

Heitowit, Janet Epstein, and Gerald Steinberg, *Science, Technology, and Society: A Guide to the Field* (Ithaca, N.Y.: Cornell University, 1976).

23. John R. Hendrix, "A Survey of Bioethics Courses in U.S. Colleges & Universities." *American Biology Teacher* 39 (February 1977): 85–92.

24. See Bibliography for examples of these materials.

25. Louis Hodges was particularly helpful to us in our examination of pre-professional ethics, as was his paper, "Applied Ethics and Pre-Professionals."

26. This general issue is discussed in greater detail in Susan Resneck Parr, "The Teaching of Ethics in Non-Ethics Courses," in Callahan and Bok, *Ethics Teaching in Higher Education.*

27. For a further, related discussion, see section III, E,1, below.

28. The general problem of undergraduate ethics is taken up in greater detail in Bernard Rosen and Arthur Caplan, *Ethics in the Undergraduate Curriculum* (Hastings-on-Hudson, N.Y.: The Hastings Center, 1980).

29. Edward B. Fiske, "Ethics Courses Now Attracting More U.S. College Students."

30. K. Danner Clouser, "Medicine, Humanities, and Integrating Perspectives," *Journal of Medical Education* 52 (November 1977). See also Robert J. Baum, *Ethics and Engineering Curricula* (Hastings-on-Hudson, N.Y.: The Hastings Center, 1980); Charles W. Powers & David Vogel, *Ethics in the Education of Business Managers* (Hastings-on-Hudson, N.Y.: The Hastings Center, 1980); and Donald P. Warwick, *The Teaching of Ethics in the Social Sciences* (Hastings-on-Hudson, N.Y.: The Hastings Center, 1980).

31. For a fuller discussion of these points see William F. May, "Professional Ethics: Setting, Terrain, and Teaching"; see also William F. May, "Notes on the Ethics of Doctors and Lawyers." (Bloomington, Indiana: The Poynter Center, Indiana University, 1977). For further readings, see Bibliography.

32. See Monroe H. Freedman, *Lawyers' Ethics in an Adversary System* (New York: Bobbs-Merrill, 1975); Robert Merton and Renée Fox, "Training for Uncertainty," in *The Student Physician,* eds. Robert Merton, George Reader, and Patricia Kendall (Cambridge, Mass.: Harvard University Press, 1969 [1957]).

33. For example, see Edmund D. Pellegrino, "Ethics and the Moral Center of the Medical Enterprise," *Bulletin of the N.Y. Academy of Medicine* 54 (1978).

34. Robert M. Veatch, "National Survey of the Teaching of Medical Ethics in Medical Schools," in *The Teaching of Medical Ethics,* eds. Robert M. Veatch, Willard Gaylin, and Councilman Morgan (Hastings-on-Hudson, N.Y.: The Hastings Center, 1973); Robert M. Veatch and Sharmon Sollitto, "Medical Ethics Teaching: Report of a National Medical School Survey," *Journal of the American Medical Association* 235 (March 8, 1976). We are particularly in-

debted to K. Danner Clouser for assisting us in our analysis of medical school ethics teaching. A more detailed discussion of the teaching of medical ethics will be found in K. Danner Clouser, *Teaching Bioethics: Strategies, Problems, and Resources* (Hastings-on-Hudson, N.Y.: The Hastings Center, 1980).

35. E.g., Georgetown University, University of Tennessee, and the University of Texas.

36. Since 1972, The Hastings Center has held annual one-week summer workshops on bioethics. A majority of the 1,200 participants to have taken part in these workshops have been university and professional school teachers. The Kennedy Center for Ethics at Georgetown University has offered a number of one-week "total immersion" workshops in bioethics, and the National Endowment for the Humanities regularly sponsors summer programs for college teachers as well as programs for physicians, health professionals, and practitioners of other professions; short courses have also been offered under the auspices of the National Science Foundation.

37. We are particularly indebted to Michael J. Kelly and Andrew Kaufman for their assistance in our analysis of the teaching of ethics in law schools. For a more detailed discussion, see Michael J. Kelly, *Legal Ethics and Legal Education* (Hastings-on-Hudson, N.Y.: The Hastings Center, 1980).

38. Standard 302 (a) (iii), *ABA Standards for the Approval of Law Schools*.

39. Stuart C. Goldberg, "1977 National Survey on Current Methods of Teaching Professionals Responsibility in Law Schools," in *Teaching Professional Responsibility: Materials and Proceedings from the National Conference*, Patrick A. Keenan, ed. (Detroit: University of Detroit Law School, 1979).

40. Ronald M. Pipkin, "Law School Instruction in Professional Responsibility: A Curricular Paradox," *1979 American Bar Foundation Research Journal*, no. 2.

41. See Bibliography for examples of this material.

42. Charles W. Powers and David Vogel were of major assistance in our study of the teaching of business ethics. For a more complete account, see Charles W. Powers and David Vogel, *The Role of Ethics in the Education of Business Managers* (Hastings-on-Hudson, N.Y.: The Hastings Center, 1980). See also Max L. Stackhouse, "Business and Ethics," *The Hastings Center Report* 7, no. 6 (December 1977).

43. Donald P. Warwick and Herbert C. Kelman provided considerable help in our study of the teaching of ethics and the social sciences. For a fuller discussion, see Donald P. Warwick, *The Teaching of Ethics in the Social Sciences* (Hastings-on-Hudson, N.Y.: The Hastings Center, 1980).

44. See Steven G. West and Steven P. Gunn, "Some Issues of Ethics and Social Psychology," *American Psychologist*, January 1978, pp. 30–38.

45. Mila Aroskar, "Ethics in the Nursing Curriculum," *Nursing Outlook* 25 (April 1977): 260–264; Mila Aroskar and Robert M. Veatch, "Ethics Teaching in Nursing Schools," *The Hastings Center Report* 7 (August 1977): 23–26.

46. Ann Davis and Mila Aroskar, *Ethical Dilemmas and Nursing Practice* (New York: Appleton-Century-Crofts, 1978).

47. Robert J. Baum was particularly helpful in our examination of the teaching of ethics in schools of engineering. For a more complete account, see Robert J. Baum, *Ethics and Engineering Curricula* (Hastings-on-Hudson, N.Y.: The Hastings Center, 1980).

48. See Bibliography.

49. Clifford G. Christians and Catherine L. Covert bore a heavy responsibility for our examination of journalism. A more detailed account will be found in their study, *Teaching Ethics in Journalism Education* (Hastings-on-Hudson, N.Y.: The Hastings Center, 1980).

50. See Bibliography.

51. Joel L. Fleishman and Bruce L. Payne were of particular help in our examination of schools of public policy and public administration. For a fuller account, see their study, *Ethical Dilemmas and the Education of Policymakers* (Hastings-on-Hudson, N.Y.: The Hastings Center, 1980). In addition, in 1977, The Hastings Center carried out a study for The Ford Foundation of "The Teaching of Ethics in Schools of Public Policy," and the results of that study were drawn upon as well. The field of ethics and public policy has been considerably strengthened by the work of the Center for Philosophy and Public Policy at the University of Maryland, directed by Peter Brown. The Center offers regular summer workshops in ethics and public policy.

52. See Bibliography.

53. The following specification of "goals" draws upon Daniel Callahan, "Goals in the Teaching of Ethics," in Callahan and Bok, *Ethics Teaching in Higher Education*.

54. Kurt Baier, *The Moral Point of View* (New York: Random House, 1966).

55. Bernard Rosen, "Goals in The Teaching of Ethics," unpublished paper presented at a meeting of The Hastings Center Project on The Teaching of Ethics.

56. Peter Caws, Thomas Green, and Ruth Macklin were of particular help in our discussions on pluralism and indoctrination. For a fuller discussion of those subjects, see Ruth Macklin, "Problems in The Teaching of Ethics," in Callahan and Bok, *Ethics Teaching in Higher Education;* See Also Peter Caws, "On the Teaching of Ethics in a Pluralistic Society," *The Hastings Center Report* 8 (October 1978). For further references, see Bibliography.

57. Peter Caws, "On the Teaching of Ethics in a Pluralistic Society," pp. 35–38.

58. This topic is discussed in greater detail in an appendix to "Goals in the Teaching of Ethics," by Daniel Callahan, in Callahan and Bok, *Ethics Teaching in Higher Education*. Cf. *The Teaching of Bioethics* (Hastings-on-Hudson, N.Y.: The Hastings Center, 1976), p. 11.

59. Arthur Caplan had a special responsibility for the subject of evaluation. For a more detailed discussion, see Arthur Caplan, "Evaluation and The Teaching of Ethics," in Callahan and Bok, *Ethics Teaching in Higher Education*. See also Mary Warnock, "Towards a Definition of Quality in Education," in R.S. Peters, ed., *The Philosophy of Education* (Oxford: Oxford University Press, 1971); and James R. Rest, "Recent Research on an Objective Test of Moral Judgment: How the Important Issues are Defined," in *Moral Development: Current Theory and Research*, D.J. DePalma and J.M. Foley, eds. (Hillsdale, New York: Erlbaum, 1975); and James R. Rest, "The Impact of Higher Education on Moral Judgment Development," Technical Report #5, Minnesota Moral Research Projects, University of Minnesota Graduate School, September, 1979.

60. Martin Trow, "Higher Education . . .," p. 25.

Bibliography

The Teaching of Ethics Project of The Hastings Center has, in addition to this report, also published a book on the teaching of ethics and eight monographs on special areas in the teaching of ethics.

1. Book

Callahan, Daniel and Bok, Sissela, eds., *Ethics Teaching in Higher Education. New York: Plenum Press, 1980.*

Contents:
 a. Douglas Sloan, "The Teaching of Ethics in the American Undergraduate Curriculum, 1876–1976"
 b. Daniel Callahan, "Goals in the Teaching of Ethics." Appendix: "Qualifications for the Teaching of Ethics"
 c. Ruth Macklin, "Problems in the Teaching of Ethics: Pluralism and Indoctrination"
 d. Thomas Lickona, "What Does Moral Psychology Have to Say to the Teacher of Ethics?"
 e. Arthur Caplan, "Evaluation and the Teaching of Ethics"
 f. Bernard Rosen, "The Teaching of Undergraduate Ethics"
 g. Susan Parr, "The Teaching of Ethics in Undergraduate Non-Ethics Courses"
 h. William F. May, "Professional Ethics: Setting, Terrain, and Teacher"
 i. Dennis Thompson, "Paternalism in Medicine, Law and Public Policy"
 j. Sissela Bok, "Whistle-blowing and Professional Responsibilities"
 k. Bibliography

2. Monographs

- Baum, Robert J. *Ethics and Engineering Curricula.* Hastings-on-Hudson, N.Y.: The Hastings Center, 1980.
- Christians, Clifford G. and Covert, Catherine L. *Teaching Ethics in Journalism Education.* Hastings-on-Hudson, N.Y.: The Hastings Center, 1980.
- Clouser, K. Danner, *Teaching Bioethics: Strategies, Problems, and Resources.* Hastings-on-Hudson, N.Y.: The Hastings Center, 1980.
- Fleishman, Joel L. and Payne, Bruce L. *Ethical Dilemmas and the Education of Policymakers.* Hastings-on-Hudson, N.Y.: The Hastings Center, 1980.
- Kelly, Michael J. *Legal Ethics and Legal Education.* Hastings-on-Hudson, N.Y.: The Hastings Center, 1980.
- Powers, Charles W. and Vogel, David. *Ethics in the Education of Business Managers.* Hastings-on-Hudson, N.Y.: The Hastings Center, 1980.
- Rosen, Bernard and Caplan, Arthur L. *Ethics in the Undergraduate Curriculum.* Hastings-on-Hudson, N.Y.: The Hastings Center, 1980.
- Warwick, Donald P. *The Teaching of Ethics in the Social Sciences.* Hastings-on-Hudson, N.Y.: The Hastings Center, 1980.

The following references are meant to provide an introduction to the topics found below. These references represent a selected list from a literature that ranges from quite extensive in some subject areas to almost nonexistent in others. Annotations have been provided only in those cases where the title may not fully reveal the contents.

I. General Articles on the Teaching of Ethics

Archambault, Reginald D. "Criteria for Success in Moral Instruction." *Harvard Educational Review* 33 (Fall 1963), pp. 472–83.

Bennett, William J. and Delattre, Edwin. "Moral Education in the Schools." *The Public Interest* no. 50 (Winter 1978), pp. 81–98.

Bereiter, Carl. "The Morality of Moral Education." *Hastings Center Report* 8:2 (April 1978), pp. 20–25.

Bok, Derek. "Can Ethics Be Taught?" *Change* 8 (October 1976), pp. 26–30.

Bok, Sissela and Callahan, Daniel. "Teaching Applied Ethics." *Radcliffe Quarterly* 69:2 (June 1979), pp. 30–33.

Callahan, Daniel. "The Rebirth of Ethics." *National Forum* 58:2 (Spring 1978), pp. 9–12.

Frankena, William. "Towards a Philosophy of Moral Education." *Harvard Educational Review* 28 (Fall 1958), pp. 300–13.

Montefiore, Alan. "Moral Philosophy and the Teaching of Morality." *Harvard Educational Review* 35 (1965), pp. 435–49.

Peters, R. S. "Moral Development and Moral Learning." *Monist* 58 (1974), pp. 541–68.

Ryle, Gilbert. "Can Virtue Be Taught?" In R. F. Dearden, P. H. Hirst, and R. S. Peters, *Education and the Development of Reason.* London: Routledge and Kegan Paul, 1972.

Trow, Martin. "Higher Education and Moral Development." *American Association of University Professors Bulletin* (Spring 1976), pp. 20–27.

Walzer, Michael. "Teaching Morality." *The New Republic* 178:23 (June 10, 1978), pp. 12–14.

II. Moral Philosophy

Baier, Kurt. *The Moral Point of View: A Rational Basis of Ethics.* New York: Random House, 1958.

Berlin, Isaiah. *Four Essays on Liberty.* Oxford: Oxford University Press, 1968.

Bok, Sissela. *Lying: Moral Choice in Public and Private Life.* New York: Pantheon Books, 1978.

Brandt, Richard B. *Ethical Theory.* Englewood Cliffs, N.J.: Prentice-Hall, 1959.

Donagan, Alan. *The Theory of Morality.* Chicago: University of Chicago Press, 1977.

Feinberg, Joel, ed. *Moral Concepts.* New York: Oxford University Press, 1969.

Frankena, William K. *Ethics.* 2nd ed. Englewood Cliffs, N.J.: Prentice-Hall, 1974.

Fried, Charles. *Right and Wrong.* Cambridge, Mass.: Harvard University Press, 1978.

Harmon, Gilbert. *The Nature of Morality.* New York: Oxford University Press, 1977.

MacIntyre, Alasdair. *A Short History of Ethics.* New York: Macmillan, 1966.

Mackie, J. L. *Ethics: Inventing Right and Wrong.* New York: Penguin, 1977.

Nozick, Robert. *Anarchy, State, and Utopia.* New York: Basic Books, 1974.

Ollman, Bertell. *Alienation: Marx's Conception of Man in Capitalist Society.* New York: Cambridge University Press, 1976.

Rachels, James, ed. *Moral Problems: A Collection of Philosophical Essays.* New York: Harper & Row, 1971.

Rawls, John. *A Theory of Justice.* Cambridge, Mass.: Harvard University Press, 1971.

Sellars, W. S. and Hospers, John, eds. *Readings in Ethical Theory.* 2nd ed. New York: Appleton-Century-Crofts, 1970.

Smart, J. J. C. and Williams, Bernard. *Utilitarianism: For and Against.* New York: Cambridge University Press, 1973.

Taylor, Paul, ed. *Problems in Moral Philosophy: An Introduction to Ethics.* 2nd ed. Belmont, California: Dickenson Publishing Co., 1971.

Toulmin, Stephen Edelston. *An Examination of the Place of Reason in Ethics.* New York: Cambridge University Press, 1950.

Williams, Bernard. *Morality: An Introduction to Ethics.* New York: Harper & Row, 1972.

III. Theological Ethics

Fox, Marvin, ed. *Modern Jewish Ethics: Theory and Practice.* Columbus, Ohio: Ohio State University Press, 1975.

Gustafson, James. *Protestant and Roman Catholic Ethics.* Chicago: University of Chicago Press, 1978.

————. *Can Ethics Be Christian?* Chicago: University of Chicago Press, 1975.

Gutierrez, Gustavo. *A Theology of Liberation.* Maryknoll, New York: Orbis Books, 1973.

Häring, Bernard. *Toward a Christian Moral Theology.* Notre Dame, Ind.: University of Notre Dame Press, 1966.

Häring, Bernard. *Morality is for Persons.* New York: Farrar, Straus & Giroux, 1970.

Kellner, Menachem Marc, ed. *Contemporary Jewish Ethics.* New York: Sanhedrin Press, 1978.

Maguire, Daniel C. *The Moral Choice.* Garden City, New York: Doubleday, 1978.

McCormick, Richard A. *Ambiguity in Moral Choice.* Milwaukee: Marquette University Press, 1973.

Niebuhr, H. Richard. *The Responsible Self.* New York: Harper & Row, 1978.

Niebuhr, Reinhold. *An Interpretation of Christian Ethics.* Cleveland: World Publishing Co., 1963 (1935).

O'Connell, Timothy E. *Principles for a Catholic Morality.* New York: Seabury Press, 1978.

Outka, Gene H. *Agape: An Ethical Analysis.* New Haven: Yale University Press, 1972.

Ramsey, Paul. *Basic Christian Ethics.* Chicago: University of Chicago Press, 1950.

Tillich, Paul. *Morality and Beyond.* New York; Harper & Row, 1963.

IV. Education and Morality

Astin, Alexander. *Four Critical Years: Effects of College on Beliefs, Attitudes and Knowledge.* San Francisco: Jossey-Bass, 1977.

Beck, C. M., Crittenden, B. S., and Sullivan, E. V. eds. *Moral Education.* Toronto: University of Toronto Press, 1971.

Bruneau, William. "A Resource Bibliography for the History of Moral Education in Western Europe 1850–1939." *Moral Education Forum* 4:3 (Fall 1979), pp. 8–15, 18–20.

Carter, Jack L. "The Anatomy of Controversy: Freedom and Responsibility for Teaching." *BioScience* 29:8 (August 1979), pp. 481–84.

Delattre, Edwin J. and Bennett, William J. "Where the Values Movement Goes Wrong." *Change* 11:1 (February 1979), pp. 38–43.

Grant, Gerald and Riesman, David. *The Perpetual Dream: Reform and Experiment in the American College.* Chicago: The University of Chicago Press, 1978.

Hall, Robert T. and Davis, John V. *Moral Education in Theory and Practice.* Buffalo, N.Y.: Prometheus Books, 1975.

Kirschenbaum, Howard, Simon, Sidney, and Howe, Leland. *Values Clarification.* New York: Hart Publishing Co., 1972.

Kohlberg, Lawrence. *Collected Papers on Moral Development and Moral Education.* Cambridge, Mass.: Center for Moral Education, Harvard University, 1973.

Langford, Glenn, ed. *New Essays in the Philosophy of Education.* London: Routledge and Kegan Paul, 1973.

Lickona, Thomas, ed. *Moral Development and Behavior.* New York: Holt, Rinehart, and Winston, 1976.

McGrath, Earl J. *Values, Liberal Education and National Destiny*. Indianapolis: Lilly Endowment, n.d.

Mischel, Theodore. *Cognitive Development and Epistemology*. New York: Academic Press, 1971.

Perry, William G. *Forms of Intellectual and Ethical Development in the College Years: A Scheme*. New York: Holt, Rinehart, and Winston, 1970.

Peters, R. S., ed. *The Philosophy of Education*. Oxford: Oxford University Press, 1971.

Rudolph, Frederick. *Curriculum: A History of the American Undergraduate Course of Study Since 1636*. San Francisco: Jossey-Bass, 1972.

Schwarzlose, Richard A. "Socratic Method Adds Zest to Ethics, Law Classes." *Journalism Educator* 33:1 (April 1978), pp. 9–24.

V. Law

Countryman, Vern, Feinman, and Schneyer. *The Lawyer in Modern Society*. Boston: Little, Brown & Co., 1976.

Feinberg, Joel and Gross, Hyman, eds. *Philosophy of Law*. Belmont, California: Dickenson Publishing Co., 1975.

Frankel, Marvin E. "The Search for Truth. An Umpireal View." *University of Pennsylvania Law Review* 123:5 (May 1975), pp. 1031–59.

Freedman, Monroe. *Lawyer's Ethics in an Adversary System*. Indianapolis, Ind.: Bobbs Merrill, 1975.

Freedman, Monroe. "Professional Responsibility of the Criminal Defense Lawyer: The Three Hardest Questions." *Michigan Law Review* 64 (June 1966), pp. 1469–84.

Freund, Paul A. "The Moral Education of the Lawyer." *Emory Law Journal* 26:1 (Winter 1977), pp. 3–12.

Gorovitz, Samuel and Miller, Bruce. *Professional Responsibility in the Law: A Curriculum Report from the Institute on Law and Ethics*. College Park, Maryland: Council for Philosophical Studies, 1977.

Hazard, Geoffrey C. *Ethics in the Practice of Law*. New Haven: Yale University Press, 1978.

Kaufman, Andrew L. *Problems in Professional Responsibility*. Boston: Little, Brown & Co., 1976.

Lawrey, Robert. "Lying, Confidentiality, and the Adversary System of Justice." *Utah Law Review* no. 4 (1977), pp. 653–94.

Meltsner, Michael and Schrag, Philip G. "Report from a CLEPR (Council on Legal Education for Professional Responsibility) Colony." *Columbia Law Review* 76:4 (May 1976), pp. 581–632.

Noonan, John T. "Professional Ethics or Personal Responsibility?" *Stanford Law Review* 29 (1977), p. 363.

Schwartz, Murray. "The Professionalism and Accountability of Lawyers." *California Law Review* 66 (1978), p. 669.

Wasserstrom, Richard A. *Morality and the Law*. Belmont, California: Wadsworth Publishing Co., 1971.

————. "Lawyers As Professionals: Some Moral Issues." *Human Rights* 5 (Fall 1975), pp. 1–24.

Weinstein, Jack. "On the Teaching of Legal Ethics." *Columbia Law Review* 72 (1972), p. 452.

————. "Educating Ethical Lawyers," *New York State Bar Journal* 47 (June 1975), pp. 260–63.

VI. Public Policy

Arendt, Hannah. "Lying in Politics." In her collection *Crisis of the Republic*. New York: Harcourt Brace Jovanovich, 1972.

Barry, Brian. *Political Argument*. London: Routledge and Kegan Paul, 1965.

Beauchamp, Tom L., ed. *Ethics and Public Policy*. Englewood Cliffs, N.J.: Prentice-Hall, 1975.

Calabresi, Guido and Bobbitt, Philip. *Tragic Choices*. New York: W. W. Norton, 1978.

Cohen, Marshall et al., eds. *Equality and Preferential Treatment*. Princeton: Princeton University Press, 1976.

Glover, Jonathan. *Causing Deaths and Saving Lives*. New York: Penguin, 1971.

Hampshire, Stuart, ed. *Public and Private Morality*. Cambridge: Cambridge University Press, 1978.

Held, Virginia. *The Public Interest and Individual Interest*. New York: Basic Books, 1970.

Jonsen, Albert and Butler, L. H. "Public Ethics and Policymaking." *Hastings Center Report* 5:3 (August 1975), pp. 19–31.

Price, David. "Public Policy and Ethics." *Hastings Center Report* 7:6 (December 1977), pp. 4–6.

Rohr, John. *Ethics for Bureaucrats: An Essay on Law and Values*. New York: Dekkar, 1978.

Self, Peter. *Econocrats and Policy Process: The Politics and Philosophy of Cost-Benefit Analysis*. London: Macmillan, 1975.

Strauss, Leo. *What is Political Philosophy?* Westport, Conn.: Greenwood, 1973 (1959).

Thurow, Lester. *Generating Inequality*. New York: Basic Books, 1975.

Tribe, Laurence. *When Values Conflict: Essays on Environmental Analysis, Discourse and Decision*. Cambridge, Mass.: Ballinger, 1976.

Walzer, Michael. *Just and Unjust Wars*. New York: Basic Books, 1977.

Walzer, Michael. "Political Action: The Problem of Dirty Hands." In *Philosophy and Public Affairs* 2:2 (Winter 1973), pp. 160–80.

Wolin, Sheldon. *Politics and Vision: Continuity and Innovation in Western Political Thought*. Boston: Little, Brown & Co., 1960. Especially chap. 10.

VII. Business

Ackerman, Robert and Bauer, Raymond, eds. *Corporate Social Responsiveness: The Modern Dilemma*. Reston, Virginia: Reston Publishing Company, Inc., 1976.

Barach, Jeffrey, Ed. *The Individual, Business, and Society*. Englewood Cliffs, N.J.: Prentice-Hall, 1977.

Beauchamp, Tom L. and Bowie, Norman, eds. *Ethical Theory and Business*. Englewood Cliffs, N.J.: Prentice-Hall, 1979.

Brenner, Steven N. and Molander, Earl A. "Is the Ethics of Business Changing?" *Harvard Business Review* (January-February 1977), pp. 57–71.

DeGeorge, Richard T., and Pichler, Joseph. *Ethics, Free Enterprise, and Public Policy: Original Essays on Moral Issues in Business*. Oxford: Oxford University Press, 1978.

Donaldson, Thomas, and Werhane, Patricia, eds. *Ethical Issues in Business. A Philosophical Approach*. Englewood Cliffs, N.J.: Prentice-Hall, 1979.

Epstein, Edwin, and Votaw, Dow, eds. *Legitimacy, Responsibility and Rationality*. Santa Monica, California: Goodyear, 1978. A collection of original essays that addresses both ethical and social issues.

Henderson, Hazel. "Should Business Tackle Society's Problems?" *Harvard Business Review* (May-June 1968), pp. 77–85.

Purcell, Theodore. "A Practical Guide to Ethics in Business," *Business and Society Review* 13 (Spring 1975), pp. 43–50.

Ermann, M. David, and Lundman, Richard J., eds. *Corporate and Governmental Deviance: Problems of Organizational Behavior In Contemporary Society.* Oxford: Oxford University Press, 1978.

Luthans, Fred and Hodgetts, Richard M., eds. *Social Issues in Business.* New York: Macmillan, 1976.

Nicholson, Edward A., Litschert, Robert J., and Anthony, William P., eds. *Business Responsibility and Social Issues.* Columbus, Ohio: Charles E. Merrill Publishing Co., 1974.

Sethi, S. Prakash. *Up Against the Corporate Wall.* Englewood Cliffs, N.J.: Prentice-Hall, 1977.

Steiner, George A. and Steiner, John F., eds. *Issues in Business and Society.* New York: Random House, 1972.

Stone, Christopher. *Where the Law Ends.* New York: Harper & Row, 1975.

VIII. Social Science

Bermant, Gordon, Kelman, Herbert, and Warwick, Donald, eds. *The Ethics of Social Intervention.* Washington, D.C.: Hemisphere Publishing Company, 1978.

Bogart, Leo. *Silent Politics: Polls and the Awareness of Public Opinion.* New York: Wiley-Interscience, 1972.

Bower, Robert T. and de Gasparis, Priscilla. *Ethics in Social Research: Protecting the Interests of Human Subjects.* New York: Praeger, 1978. More than half of this book is devoted to an annotated bibliography on ethics in social research.

Denzin, N. K. and Erikson, Kai. "On the Ethics of Disguised Observation." *Social Problems* 15 (1968), pp. 502–6.

Diener, Edward and Crandall, Rick. *Ethics in Social and Behavioral Research.* Chicago: University of Chicago Press, 1978.

Erikson, Kai T. "A Comment on Disguised Observation in Sociology." *Social Problems* 16 (1967), pp. 366–73.

Gouldner, Alvin. "Anti-Minotaur: The Myth of Value-free Sociology." *Social Problems* 9 (1962), pp. 199–213.

Katz, Jay. *Experimentation with Human Beings: The Authority of the Investigator, Subject, Professions, and State in the Human Experimentation Process.* New York: Russell Sage Foundation, 1972.

Kelman, Herb. *A Time to Speak: On Human Values and Social Research.* San Francisco: Jossey-Bass, 1968.

Macrae, Duncan, Jr. *The Social Function of Social Science.* New Haven: Yale University Press, 1976.

Mead, Margaret. "Research with Human Beings: A Model Derived from Anthropological Field Practice." *Daedelus* 98 (1969), pp. 361–86.

Rivlin, Alice M. and Timpane, P. Michael, eds. *Ethical and Legal Issues of Social Experimentation.* Washington, D.C.: Brookings Institution, 1975.

Ruebhausen, O. M. and Brim, O. G., Jr. "Privacy and Behavioral Research." *Columbia Law Review* 65 (1965).

Sjoberg, Gideon, ed. *Ethics, Politics, and Social Research.* San Francisco: Jossey-Bass, 1968.

IX. Engineering

Baum, Robert J. and Flores, Albert W. (eds.), *Ethical Problems in Engineering.* Troy, N.Y.: Rensselaer Polytechnic Institute, Human Dimensions Center, 1978.

Bonnell, John A., ed. *A Guide for Developing Courses in Engineering.* NSPE Publication #2010, Washington, D.C.: National Society of Professional Engineers, 1976.

Ethics, Professionalism & Maintaining Competence: Proceedings of a Conference held at the Ohio State University, March 10–11, 1977. New York: American Society of Civil Engineers, 1977.

Florman, Samuel. *The Existential Pleasures of Engineering.* New York: St. Martin's Press, 1976. In this volume, Florman explores the nature of the engineering profession and its obligations to society.

Fruchtbaum, Harold ed., *The Social Responsibility of Engineers.* (Annals of the New York Academy of Sciences 196, pt. 10), New York: Scholarly Reprints, 1973.

Layton, Edwin T., Jr. *Revolt of the Engineers: Social Responsibility and the American Engineering Profession.* Cleveland: Case Western Reserve Press, 1971.

Oldenquist, Andrew G. and Slouter, Edward E. "Proposed: A Single Code of Ethics for All Engineers" *Professional Engineer* 49:5 (May 1979), pp. 8–11.

Perrucci, Robert and Gerstl, Joel E. *Profession Without Community: Engineers in American Society.* New York: Random House, 1969.

Weil, Vivian M. "Moral Issues in Engineering: An Engineering School Instructional Approach." *Professional Engineer* (October, 1977), pp. 45–47.

XI. Journalism

Carty, James W. "Ethics: A Lost Concept." *The Collegiate Journalist* 8 (Spring 1971), pp. 11–18.

Christians, Clifford G. "Fifty Years of Scholarship in Media Ethics." *Journal of Communication* 27 (Autumn 1977), pp. 19–29.

Christians, Clifford G. "Problem-Solving in a Mass-Media Course." *Communications Education* 28 (May 1979), pp. 139–43. Describes a teaching methodology aimed at helping students develop analytic skills.

Diggs, Bernard J. "Persuasion and Ethics." *The Quarterly Journal of Speech* 50:4 (December 1974), pp. 359–73.

Kelley, Frank K. "Ethics of Journalism in a Century of Change." *Nieman Reports* 22 (June 1968), pp. 12–15.

Rivers, William L. and Schramm, Wilbur. *Responsibility in Mass Communication*. Rev. ed. New York: Harper & Row (1957) 1969.

Rubin, Bernard, ed. *Questioning Media Ethics*. New York: Praeger Special Studies, 1978.

Sanders, Keith and Won Chang. "Freebies: Achille's Heel of Journalism" Ethics. Columbia, Missouri: Freedom of Information Foundation, University of Missouri, March 1977. An investigation of professional reactions to ethics codes.

Swain, Bruce M. *Reporter's Ethics*. Ames, Iowa: Iowa State University Press, 1978.

Thayer, Lee, ed. *Communication: Ethical and Moral Issues*. New York: Gordon and Breach, 1973.

Thomson, James C. "Journalistic Ethics: Some Probings by a Media Keeper." Bloomington, Ind.: The Poynter Center, Indiana University Press, January 1978.

XII. Bioethics

Aroskar, Mila A. "Ethics in the Nursing Curriculum." *Nursing Outlook* 25 (April 1977), pp. 260–64.

———— and Veatch, Robert. "Ethics Teaching in Nursing Schools." *Hastings Center Report* 7 (August 1977), pp. 23–26.

Beauchamp, Tom L. and Childress, James F. *Principles of Biomedical Ethics*. New York: Oxford University Press, 1979.

———— and Walters, LeRoy, eds. *Contemporary Issues in Bioethics*. Belmont, California: Dickenson Publishing Co., 1978.

Davis, Ann and Aroskar, Mila. *Ethical Dilemmas and Nursing Practice*. New York: Appleton-Century-Crofts, 1978.

Gorovitz, Samuel, et al., eds. *Moral Problems in Medicine*. Englewood Cliffs, N.J.: Prentice-Hall, 1976.

Gustafson, James M. *The Contributions of Theology to Medical Ethics*. Milwaukee, Wisc.: Marquette University Theology Department, 1975.

Heitowit, Ezra D., Epstein, Janet, and Steinberg, Gerald. *Science, Technology, and Society: A Guide to the Field*. Ithaca, N.Y.: Cornell University Press, 1976.

Hendrix, Jon R. "A Survey of Bioethics Courses in U.S. Colleges and Universities." *American Biology Teacher* 39 (Feb. 1977), pp. 85–92.

Humber, James M. and Almeder, Robert F., eds. *Biomedical Ethics and the Law*. New York: Plenum Press, 1976.

Hunt, Robert and Arras, John, eds. *Ethical Issues in Modern Medicine*. Palo Alto, California: Mayfield Publishing Company, 1977.

Jakobovits, Immanuel. *Jewish Medical Ethics*. New York: Bloch Publishing Co., 1959.

Purtilo, Ruth B. "Ethics Teaching in Allied Health Fields." *The Hastings Center Report* 8:2 (April 1978), pp. 14–16.

Ramsey, Paul. *The Patient as Person*. New Haven: Yale University Press, 1970.

Reich, Warren T., editor-in-chief. *Encyclopedia of Bioethics*. New York: The Free Press, 1978.

Sollitto, Sharmon, Veatch, Robert, and Singer, Ira. *Bibliography of Society, Ethics, and the Life Sciences 1979–80*. Hastings-on-Hudson, N.Y.: The Hastings Center, 1979.

The Teaching of Bioethics: Report of the Commission on the Teaching of Bioethics. Hastings-on-Hudson, N.Y.: Institute of Society, Ethics and the Life Sciences, 1976.

Veatch, Robert. *Case Studies in Medical Ethics*. Cambridge, Mass.: Harvard University Press, 1977.

Walters, Le Roy, ed. *Bibliography of Bioethics*. Detroit: Gale Research Co., 1973–.

XIII. Professional Ethics

Bledstein, Burton. *The Culture of Professionalism.* New York: W. W. Norton, 1976.

Boley, Bruno A. *Crossfire in Professional Education: Students, the Professions, and Society.* New York: Pergamon Press, 1977.

Collins, Randall, *The Credential Society.* New York: The Academic Press, 1979.

Freidson, Eliot. *Professional Dominance: The Social Structure of Medical Care.* New York: Atherton Press, Inc., 1970.

Larson, Magali S., *The Rise of Professionalism.* Berkeley: University of California Press, 1977.

Merton, Robert K., ed. *Authority and the Individual.* New York: Arno Press, 1974.